Money and Time-Saving Household
HINTS

Revised & Enlarged

Volume I of the Best-Selling Household Hints Series

*Over 1,000 great ideas from the readers of
The Leader-Post to use in your home and yard*

Household Hints, Volume 1, Revised & Enlarged
By The Leader-Post Carrier Foundation Inc.

Sixth Printing — June, 1998

Canadian Cataloguing in Publication Data
Main entry under title:

Household hints

   Includes index.
   ISBN 1-895292-39-5

1. Home economics.   I. Leader-post.

TX158.H68 1988   640   C88-0948140-7

Illustrations by
Yves Noblet
Wendy Anderson

Designed, Printed and Produced in Canada by:
Centax Books, A Division of PrintWest Communications Ltd.
Publishing Director – Margo Embury
1150 Eighth Avenue, Regina, Saskatchewan, Canada S4R 1C0
(306) 525-2304   Fax: (306) 757-2439

TABLE OF CONTENTS

IMPORTANT NOTICE:

The "household tips" described in this publication have not been tested by the Leader-Post Carrier Foundation Inc. The Leader-Post Carrier Foundation Inc. gives no warranty as to the usefulness, or as to the safety, of the suggestions which follow. Any problems arising from the use of these tips are the responsibility of the user of the tip. Use of these recommendations is solely the decision of the reader. Every user assumes all risks of injury or damage of whatsoever kind which may result from the implementation of any and all suggestions herein. Readers are warned that the combination of tips involving the use of chemicals or chemical agents may be dangerous.

TABLE OF CONTENTS

Leader Post
Carrier Foundation

The Leader-Post Carrier Foundation Inc. was established by The Leader-Post in tribute of the service provided by past and present carriers of the newspaper. Its aim is to provide financial support to educational and humanitarian needs in Saskatchewan. While it is named in honour of carriers, help is open to the public at large throughout Saskatchewan.

The Foundation is funded by contributions from the public and corporations, but primarily through the proceeds of special projects organized on behalf of the Foundation by The Leader-Post.

Not only will these household hints help you, but the proceeds from the sale of this book will help the work of The Leader-Post Carrier Foundation.

HINTS

1 Welcome to "Money and Time-Saving Household Hints", this first hint will help you to use this book more effectively.

— Make it accessible! Keep "Household Hints" in the kitchen or on a bookshelf where it is available to every member of the family.

— Use the index! Here is the key to your problem solving. Look under CLEANING for help in cleaning everything from bathrooms to brass to piano keys to silk flowers to wood panelling. There are also specific cleaning hints under BLOOD STAINS and CARPETS and LAUNDRY. The CARPETS entry also gives hints for getting out those dents when you rearrange the furniture.

Grandma can check the index under ARTHRITIS to find a hint to help her write more easily.

Teenagers can look under BLEMISHES, and BREATH to find hints that will help them fade zits and get rid of onion breath when they have a hot date.

Children can check under BANDAGES, PLAYDOUGH and POPCORN to find hints that will ensure painless bandage removal, easy-to-make playdough and fluffier popcorn.

Handymen can look under FURNITURE and GREASE and ENERGY-SAVING to find hints that will help them remove watermarks or burns from furniture, remove grease from concrete, carpets and wallpaper and save on power and fuel bills.

Cooks can check under DUMPLINGS and HONEY and VEGETABLES to find hints that will give lighter dumplings, how to use honey in baking and how to recrisp and store vegetables.

NEWSPAPERS

2 Read the newspaper. You'll always have something interesting to talk about with friends and family.

3 Purchase The Leader-Post everyday. Besides keeping you abreast of what is happening, the coupons in the paper can save you money when shopping.

4 One reader suggests putting coupons from the paper in an envelope and placing it in your purse or car so you always have them handy.

5 When you come upon coupons in The Leader-Post, apply them to the items when those items are on sale for maximum coupon benefits.

6 For a baby gift, circle the baby's birth announcement in the newspaper with a red felt and use that page as gift wrap, making certain the announcement is in a strategic position on the package.

7 Save the colored comics from The Leader-Post Weekender to wrap children's birthday gifts.

8 Color pages in The Leader-Post make ideal gift wrap. For an added touch, make ribbons and bows out of cloth leftover from sewing projects. Use pinking shears and cut strips one to three inches in width for the ribbon and bows.

9   Instead of trudging to the corner store daily for your copy of The Leader-Post, subscribe to it and it will arrive daily. You'll pay less per copy as well.

10 When preparing a cake for baking, spread newspapers on the cupboard. When the cake is mixed and in the pan, remove newspaper and there is no mess to clean up.

11 Crushed newspapers are great for shining windows.

12 To clean glass tables and chrome fixtures, use old newspapers, dampened with water. Glass and chrome will shine and there will be no streaking or lint left behind.

13 When painting around windows, wet newspapers and apply to the glass. Then, paint and splatter as you please.

14 Fill in cracks with newspaper or steel wool before finishing off with plaster.

15 Save your old newspapers for the fireplace. Take several and wrap tightly into a roll, wrap with wire and use to replace commerical fireplace logs or wood.

16 When you change your cat's litter pan, use newspaper for liners. It absorbs the odors and makes the litter last a little longer.

NEWSPAPERS

FOOD

17 Instead of using sugar in your tea, dissove old-fashioned lemon drops or hard mint candy in the brew. They melt quickly and give the tea a clean tangy flavor.

18 The flavor of tea can be enhanced by placing a thoroughly dried orange peel in the tea tin.

19 Leftover apple, orange or lemon rind can be put in your tea. It adds flavor and aroma.

20 The flavor of ground coffee will keep better if you store opened coffee in tightly-covered container in the refrigerator.

21 If you use some form of purified water, coffee will taste better and the life of your coffee maker will be prolonged.

22 Pennies placed under the pot in the drip coffee maker will prevent scum from forming on the coffee and you won't have to throw out any coffee.

23 To add flavor to coffee, add vanilla or almond extract to the water as the coffee brews.

24 Cool leftover coffee immediately, cover with tight lid and refrigerate. It warms up beautifully in the microwave.

25 Freeze leftover coffee in ice-cube trays. The cubes can be used in milk or eggnog. Coffee cubes are also great to place in too-hot coffee.

26 Scum won't form on the top of hot chocolate if you beat the drink until frothy immediately after preparation.

27 Mix a 12-ounce can of frozen orange juice in a three-quart pitcher, add one cup of powdered orange drink mix. Fill the pitcher to the brim with cold water and stir until dissolved. The powder gives the drink sweetness and the frozen juice gives it body.

28 Freeze clusters of grapes to float in punches. They keep the punch cold and add a lovely garnish.

29 When making punch, make ice cubes out of punch, then you can keep the punch cold without diluting it.

30 For cocktails, freeze lemon peel twists in party ice cubes — looks attractive and adds a tangy flavor.

31 When entertaining, serve hot cider and other hot drinks from a slow cooker on a low setting. This way, the liquid will remain warm as long as you wish.

32 Use canning funnels to fill a thermos bottle without spills.

33 To make butter go farther and spread easier, leave butter at room temperature, use electric beater and whip to twice its volume.

34 Soften hard butter for sandwiches by inverting a warmed soup bowl over it.

35 Prevent butter from burning when sautéing by adding a small amount of olive or vegetable oil. Butter alone burns easily, but the combination of the two does not. Vegetables and meats will be golden brown.

36 Blend cottage cheese in a blender until it's smooth, then you can use it in dips, instead of sour cream.

37 Cottage cheese will keep twice as long if you store the carton upside down.

38 For 1 cup of buttermilk, substitute 1/4 cup whole milk plus 3/4 cup yogurt or add 1/2 teaspoon baking powder to 1 cup of milk.

FOOD

FOOD

39 If you want to make your own sour cream, add three or four drops of lemon juice to ¾ cup whipping cream and leave it at room temperature for 30 minutes.

40 Before adding sour cream to a sauce which must boil, stir 1 tsp. of flour into the cream. The sauce can boil and the flour will prevent the sour cream from curdling.

41 When you buy bulk cheese, put it in a Tupperware container with a lid which can be burped. Place a paper towel which has been dampened with vinegar in the container. More vinegar can be added once a week to keep the cheese fresh for a month or longer.

42 Cheese wrapped in a cloth which has been dampened with vinegar will keep fresh and free from mold.

43 Mold on cheese can be prevented by storing the cheese in a covered container with a lump or two of sugar. This also keeps the cheese moist.

44 After you cut a piece of cheese, butter the edge of the remainder which is to be stored. It will be less likely to dry out and lose its consistency.

45 Grate leftover pieces of cheese together. Use for a cheese ball or serve over spaghetti.

46 Instead of throwing moldy cheese away, take a knife or cheese slicer, dip it in vinegar and slice off the mold. Dip the knife in vinegar after each slice made. The vinegar keeps the mold from coming back.

47 When boiling milk, first rinse pan with cold water to avoid boil overs.

48 To prevent milk from burning, sprinkle one tsp. of sugar over milk before heating. Do not stir.

49 Always keep powdered milk handy, in case you run out of fresh milk.

50 Always use skim milk powder in your cooking.

51 Use powdered skim milk in tea and coffee instead of edible oil products.

52 Save time and money, buy whole milk in bags of 3. It's cheaper than cartons and you don't have to run to the store so often. Mix up one jug of skim milk from powder, then fill a container with half commercial whole milk and half skim — better flavor; less fat, lots of nutrients.

53 You can make your own sweetened condensed milk and save a small fortune. The following makes 12 oz. and can be used in any recipe calling for this type of milk: Mix in blender for one minute ¼ cup hot water and ¾ cup granulated sugar. While continuing to blend slowly, add 1¼ cup dry skim milk powder. Refrigerate for 24 hours to develop the flavor. Do not store more than one week.

54 Seven drops of lemon juice added to two cups of cream before whipping will cause it to whip up in less than half the normal time.

55 For best results when whipping fresh cream, chill the bowl, beaters and cream before whipping.

56 If cream refuses to whip, add one egg white.

57 Add honey to whipped cream instead of sugar. It adds a sweet flavor and whipped cream stays firm longer.

FOOD

FOOD

58 Icing sugar used, instead of granulated sugar, in making whipped cream will prevent separation if the cream has to sit for a while.

59 To stop whipped cream from separating, add ¼ tsp. dissolved, unflavored gelatin for every cup of cream.

60 When whipping cream, to avoid splatters set the bowl in the sink and whip. All the splatters are in the sink and there's no mess to clean.

61 When whipping cream in an electric mixer, place a tea towel over your mixer to completely cover the mixer and bowl. The tea towel will catch any splattering and will keep you and your kitchen clean.

62 Spoon dabs of leftover whipped cream onto wax paper and place in the freezer. When they're frozen, place in a plastic bag and keep in the freezer to use for dessert toppings. They will thaw in 10-15 minutes.

63 Whip evaporated milk instead of cream. Place can of evaporated milk in freezer until partially frozen. Pour contents into cold bowl, add one tbsp. lemon juice to ⅔ cup milk and whip.

64 To add fresh fruit flavor to yogurt, buy plain yogurt and mix with any fresh fruit in a blender.

65 To hard cook eggs, place in a pan of cold water to cover. Bring to a boil and remove the pan from the heat. Cover and let stand 20 minutes. Immediately rinse in cold water. The eggs will be tender, the yolk will be an even yellow and there will be no grey ring.

66 Keep yolks centred in eggs by stirring the water while cooking hard-boiled eggs.

67 When boiling eggs, add one tsp. vinegar to water, to prevent cracking.

68 Before boiling a cracked egg, rub moistened salt over the shell. This prevents the white from running out.

69 Cracked Eggs: When boiling eggs, add 1 tsp. salt to the water. This will help close the cracks.

70 When eggs crack during boiling, add a little vinegar to the water to help seal the crack.

71 The yolks of eggs, left over when baking requires whites only, can be dropped into a pan of boiling and salted water. When cooked, they are ready to add to a salad.

72 Hard-boiled eggs for use in egg salad are easily mashed with a pastry blender.

73 When slicing hard-cooked eggs, wet the knife before each cut to keep the yolk from crumbling.

74 Bread crumbs added to scrambled eggs will improve the flavor and make them go further.

75 For fluffier omelettes, add a pinch of cornstarch before beating.

76 To ensure a white film over the yolk when frying eggs, add a few drops of water to the pan and cover with a lid.

77 To separate the whites of an egg from the yolk, break the egg into a funnel. The white will slip through, but the yolk will stay in the funnel.

78 If a bit of egg yolk gets into the whites you've just separated, touch the yolk with a damp cloth. It will pick up the yolk quickly and cleanly.

FOOD

FOOD

79 Egg whites will whip faster and to greater volume when brought to room temperature before beating.

80 Add one tsp. cold water for each egg white before beating and you will have double the volume.

81 One tsp. vinegar and one tsp. baking soda dissolved together will take the place of one egg when making a cake.

82 If you run one egg short in the middle of a recipe, substitute one tsp. cornstarch and one tsp. vinegar. The liquid in the recipe should then be increased by three or four tbsp. (NOTE: This will only work for one egg, no more.)

83 When cleaning green vegetables, add a handful of salt to the second water. The sand from the vegetables will sink to the bottom of the pan so another rinsing will make vegetables thoroughly clean.

84 A little vinegar added to the water in which you are soaking slightly-wilted vegetables will make them crisp and fresh.

85 Line bottom of the refrigerator vegetable compartment with paper towels. It absorbs moisture and keeps fruit and vegetables fresh longer.

86 Place a dry sponge in the vegetable compartment of the refrigerator. It will help prevent mildew and food spoilage, as it absorbs excess moisture.

87 To keep a vegetable salad fresh, if it must stand before serving, place an inverted saucer in bottom of bowl before filling with salad.

88 Wash salad vegetables before storing. It saves time and spoilage as they are easier to use when you are preparing a meal and you tend to use them more often.

89 Make your own salad dressings — they are one-third the cost of brand-name dressings.

90 Keep crispness and nutrients in your vegetables by cooking them in a vegetable steamer.

91 To keep vegetables colorful, add a pinch of baking soda to the cooking water.

92 To restore fresh flavor to frozen vegetables, pour boiling water over them to rinse away all traces of the frozen water.

93 To store asparagus in the refrigerator, for no more than a day or two, first trim the stem ends slightly and wrap the ends in wet paper towels.

94 Broccoli stalks of varying sizes can be cooked in the same length of time by making an X incision from top to bottom through stems.

95 Place a heel of bread on top of cabbage then cover and cook. There will be no odor.

96 To eliminate cabbage odor from cooking cabbage, drop a whole walnut into the boiling water.

97 When cooking cabbage, add a pinch of soda. It eliminates the odor and also keeps the cabbage green.

98 While cooking vegetables which give off an unpleasant odor, simmer a small pan of vinegar on top of the stove.

99 When making cabbage rolls, instead of steaming cabbage before pulling the leaves apart, place whole head of cabbage in the freezer until frozen solid. Then allow cabbage to thaw and you will find the leaves are easy to pull apart and they are soft and easy to work with.

FOOD

FOOD

100 To keep cauliflower white add two to three tbsp. of milk to the cooking water.

101 Before storing in the refrigerator, soak celery in cold water to which lemon juice has been added. It won't turn brown.

102 Make your own celery salt by drying celery leaves thoroughly. Crush them to a powder or rub them through a sieve and mix with salt.

103 For the best tasting corn on the cob, when removing outer leaves save the tender leaves next to the cob. Place these leaves on the bottom of the pot, add cobs, water to cover cobs and one tbsp. salt. Bring to a boil and simmer 20 minutes.

104 Corn on the cob tastes best when frozen without removing the "natural wrap". Break cobs off corn stalks, remove only coarse outer leaves, pack in plastic bags and place in the freezer.

105 Garlic will peel more easily if you put it in hot water for a few minutes to loosen the skin.

106 Store garlic cloves in cooking oil. They will never dry out and the garlic-flavored oil can be used for cooking.

107 Use old knee-high hose to dry and store garlic in a cool dry place.

108 To keep garlic longer, put the cloves in the freezer. When ready to use, peel and chop before the cloves thaw.

109 Lettuce will not go rusty if you remove its core. Bang the lettuce head on the kitchen counter and the core should twist out.

110 Lettuce keeps longer stored in a brown paper bag or on a paper towel in the produce drawer of your refrigerator.

111 Lettuce will not discolor so quickly if you line the bottom of your crisper with paper towels. The paper absorbs the excess moisture, keeping fruits and vegetables fresh for a longer period of time.

112 If lettuce has wilted, take out the core, soak in hot water, then quickly drain and put in plastic bag and refrigerate. After it's cold, you'll have fresh lettuce.

113 Always tear lettuce — cutting causes the edges to turn brown.

114 Cover fresh mushrooms with a dampened paper towel and refrigerate. They will keep fresh for several days.

115 When using mushrooms in any recipe, add a little lemon juice to bring out their flavor.

116 You don't need a food processor to get perfectly sliced mushrooms. Use an inexpensive egg slicer.

117 To keep eyes from running when peeling onions, soak the onions in cold water for five to 10 minutes and keep them under the cold water tap while you peel them.

118 Before peeling or slicing onions, place them in the freezer for a while to eliminate watery eyes.

119 To avoid tears and save on facial tissues when peeling, cutting or slicing onions, place a small piece of bread on the tip of the knife blade.

FOOD

FOOD

120 To prevent tears when peeling and chopping onions, hold a slice of bread under your chin. The bread absorbs the odors.

121 When peeling onions, chew gum and there will be no tears.

122 Leftover onion will keep longer when the root end is left intact. Use the top part first.

123 Dry parsley in the microwave and store for future use.

124 Coat peppers with olive oil before stuffing and baking them. They will keep their original color.

125 Trim ⅛-inch slice from both ends of cucumbers before making into pickles. The ends contain enzymes which may cause pickles to soften.

126 Save pickle juice. Slice unwaxed cucumbers into thin strips and refrigerate in the juice for four days. Then they are ready to enjoy.

127 Never throw away pickle juice after using all the pickles in a jar. It's great for adding to devilled eggs, coleslaw and potato salad.

128 A piece of horseradish placed in a jar of pickles will keep the vinegar from losing its strength. The pickles will not become soft or moldy.

129 When you are cleaning out your garden, wash your carrots in your automatic washer, cold water and gentle cycle. Remove carrots, dry and store in plastic bags in the refrigerator or cool place. Works great!

130 Put a few apples in with your potatoes. It keeps the potatoes from sprouting.

131 Peeled potatoes will last three or four days in the refrigerator if a few drops of vinegar are added to the water.

132 Boil potatoes with the skins on. Skins will slide off easily when the potatoes are done and you will retain a lot of the natural food value of the potatoes.

133 To improve the flavor of old potatoes, add a little sugar to the water in which they are boiled.

134 To boil old potatoes, add one tsp. vinegar to the boiling water so that they will not turn dark.

135 If dinner is getting cold, keep potatoes warm by placing the pot in a pan of hot water.

136 For fluffy mashed potatoes, add ½ tsp. baking powder to the potatoes, milk and butter. Let sit a few minutes before serving.

137 To add zip to mashed potatoes, add cooked onion and top with grated cheese or nutmeg.

138 You can cut the baking time of potatoes in half by letting them stand in boiling water for 15 minutes before popping them in the oven.

139 Reheat leftover baked potatoes instead of discarding them. Dip the potatoes in warm water, then bake at 250°F until heated through.

140 Potato Slicing: Potatoes or cheese will slice much more easily if the knife is warm.

141 About five minutes before rice is cooked, place a small absorbent towel under the pot lid. Continue cooking. The rice will be dry and fluffy.

142 To reheat leftover rice, line a vegetable steamer with a basket-like coffee filter and warm over boiling water. The grains stay in the basket and do not get mushy.

FOOD

FOOD

143 Add a few drops of lemon juice to rice when cooking. It makes rice white and keeps the grains whole.

144 Apples stored with green tomatoes will hasten the ripening process.

145 Tomatoes and cucumbers taste best when stored at room temperature.

146 Instead of adding sugar to sweeten homemade tomato sauce, grate a carrot into the sauce. Lower on calories, too.

147 To prepare a quick and delicious sauce for vegetables, simply whisk a few tablespoons of mayonnaise into the cooking liquid from the vegetables and season to taste.

148 Having trouble finding the right spice? Arrange spices in alphabetical order.

149 Put a few grains of rice in the salt shaker to keep moisture from caking the salt.

150 Save foil margarine wrappers to wrap potatoes for baking. They'll be deliciously crunchy.

151 Place unripened fruit in a plastic bag along with ripe fruit. Ripe fruit exudes a natural gas which speeds up ripening of other fruit.

152 To ripen peaches, pears or tomatoes quickly, place in a brown paper bag with a ripe apple. Poke a hole in the bag and put in a cool, dark place. The apple will give off ethylene gas and cause the other fruit to ripen.

153 When cooking apples, a pinch of salt will make them more tender and add flavor.

154 To ripen green bananas, wrap them in a wet towel and place them in a brown paper bag.

155 If you have more bananas than you can eat, peel, mash them with a dash of lemon juice and freeze in airtight containers for up to six months. Use, defrosted, in recipes which call for ripe bananas.

156 To keep bananas from getting overripe, put them in a white garbage bag, twist tie shut and place in the crisper of your refrigerator. They'll keep for a week or more.

157 If you are storing cantaloupes in the refrigerator, wrap or cover them so that the melon flavor and scent stay inside the fruit and are not transfered to other foods in the refrigerator.

158 To keep fruit from discoloring, sprinkle with lemon or pineapple juice.

159 When freezing fresh fruits or berries which don't have to be blanched, place them on a cookie sheet and freeze. When frozen, remove them from the cookie sheet and place in freezer bags or containers and put back in freezer. This prevents the fruits and berries from becoming mushy and you can remove the amount you need, without having to thaw the whole container at once.

160 Lemons will keep in the refrigerator for a month if you put them in a sterilized jar and cover them with cold water. Seal tightly with rubber-ringed lid.

161 A cut lemon may be kept longer by smearing the cut surface with the white of an egg.

162 If you only use a small piece of lemon or lime at a time, cut them into quarters and freeze them in a plastic freezer bag. They will always be available when you need them.

FOOD

FOOD

163 After using a lemon, store the remaining portion in the freezer.

164 To get just a little juice out of a citrus fruit, puncture one end with a skewer and squeeze out as much as needed. Seal fruit in plastic wrap and refrigerate.

165 To get more juice out of a lemon, heat it in a microwave before squeezing.

166 Lemons and oranges submerged in hot water for 15 minutes, then rolled on a hard surface with your hand before squeezing, will yield almost twice the amount of juice.

167 Soak oranges in boiling water for five minutes before peeling. The peel and all white pulp will come off easily.

168 To almost double the amount of juice you get from oranges, store at room temperature.

169 Vitamin C in orange juice is destroyed by exposure to air. To prevent this, slowly stir water into frozen orange juice and store in covered container.

170 Save tangerine peels and dry by laying peels loosely on a cookie sheet with the insides facing up. When dry, buzz the dried pieces in a blender and use in recipes calling for orange peel.

171 Dried orange and grapefruit peels and rind make good fuel in a fireplace and give off a lovely aroma as they burn.

172 Use a V-shaped juice can opener to remove stems from strawberries.

173 When adding pineapple to gelatin, always use cooked or canned pineapple. Raw pineapple prevents the gelatin from setting.

174 Freeze the juices from canned fruits and save until you have enough to combine with flavored or unflavored gelatin to make a dessert or salad.

175 Add a pinch of salt to Jell-o to improve flavor.

176 Metal jelly molds chill faster than glass molds.

177 Rinse your gelatin mold in cold water, then coat with oil before putting salad ingredients into the mold. It will unmold easily.

178 Grease the threads on syrup bottles to keep syrup from running down the bottle.

179 When using honey in a recipe, run hot water over your measuring spoon or measuring cup first. The honey will then slide out easily.

180 If honey has crystallized, place in microwave for 10-60 seconds (depending on amount). It will come out fresh and ready to use.

181 If you rub the bottom of your preserving kettle with a little oil, your jam will not burn. The oil leaves no taste.

182 If you do any preserving, save all of your empty jars with self-sealing lids. They will seal several times.

183 Add vinegar to hard-water in the water bath at canning time to avoid the hardwater deposit on sealers.

184 When sealing jelly jars with wax, before the wax hardens put a piece of string down in the wax. When removing the wax, just pull the string.

FOOD

FOOD

185 When you open a new bottle of ketchup, insert a straw and push to bottom of the bottle. Remove the straw and you will find that the ketchup will flow easily.

186 Save all small bits of jams and jellies in one jar. Melt and use as a basting sauce for ham, chicken or lamb.

187 If you have a damp storage area, wipe the outsides of your filled canning jars with white vinegar to keep mold away.

188 Use an empty, well-cleaned detergent bottle to store cooking oil. Just squirt the oil into the pan.

189 Add one tbsp. cooking oil to a bottle of cooking wine to prevent it from going sour.

190 Don't throw away leftover wine or wine that has begun to go off. Boil it down by half, bottle and refrigerate, then use for cooking.

191 Buy spaghetti sauce on sale and use as sauce when making pizzas.

192 To prevent any boiling-over mishaps, grease the inside rim of the pot.

193 Add one tsp. of butter or margarine to macaroni, spaghetti, soup etc. to stop from boiling over.

194 Before opening a can of soup, shake can and open bottom end. Soup will slide out easily.

195 Finely grated cheese, added to thin soup, improves the flavor immensely.

196 Unpeeled potatoes add flavor, color and nutrients to stews.

197 Save leftover vegetables in a container in the freezer and use them in soups.

198 Save any leftover vegetables and the cooking water from these vegetables in a container. Place in your freezer and add leftover vegetables as you have them. When the container is full, use the contents for making soups.

199 To make soup go further, add noodles, macaroni, barley, rice or diced potatoes.

200 To cut meat costs, serve soups, stews, casseroles, etc. with lots of dried peas, beans and lentils.

201 To thicken soup, add one tbsp. (or more) of instant potato.

202 To thicken homemade soup, add a handful of rolled oats or wheat flakes.

203 If your homemade soup is too salty, drop a raw potato in the pot and remove potato before serving.

204 Fat on the top of soup or stew can be removed easily by dropping three or four ice cubes in the pot. The fat will stick to the ice cubes and the cubes can then be scooped out.

205 Take the grease off soup or gravy by swishing a lettuce leaf gently and slowly over the surface. The lettuce will absorb the grease.

206 Pour leftover soup into ice cube trays and freeze. Remove cubes and store in plastic bags. To use, just thaw as many cubes as needed.

207 Instead of expensive smoked salmon, substitute canned salmon mixed with freshly ground pepper and a squeeze of lemon juice.

208 When using canned shrimp, prechill and they will hold their shape and texture better. Always rinse well in cold water before using.

209 It's easier to skin a frozen fish than a fresh one, so you might find it convenient to freeze fresh fish before skinning.

210 Thaw frozen fish in milk and it will taste like fresh fish.

211 Use up all those broken crackers by rolling with a rolling pin and using the crumbs for coating fish and chops.

212 Add lemon juice to shortening when frying fish. This eliminates smoke and odor.

FOOD

FOOD

213 After cooking fish, wash the pan with vinegar to remove fishy odor.

214 To keep lard from splattering while frying, sprinkle in a little salt.

215 Spray your barbecue grill with vegetable oil before barbecuing to make cleanup easier.

216 Use aluminum containers, from fast-food orders, to cook meats on the barbecue — no burning and they last forever.

217 After cleaning your wok, dry and spray with vegetable oil. This prevents rust.

218 Consider the cost per serving, not per pound, when buying meat. A boneless cut may be cheapest.

219 Separate bacon slices easily by heating the package in the microwave, on high, for 25-30 seconds.

220 Bacon slices will separate smoothly if you slip a pizza cutter between them.

221 To keep bacon from curling, dip in cold water and nick edges before cooking.

222 Place a large sheet of tinfoil on a baking sheet. Cover it with bacon strips and broil for approximately 10 minutes. This saves cooking and cleanup time since you just throw the foil away.

223 Sausage will shrink less and not break open if boiled about five minutes before frying.

224 Prevent sausage from bursting open and spattering, by piercing the skins with a fork before and during cooking.

225 If you find ham too salty, bake partially, then drain off juices, pour a small bottle of ginger ale over ham and bake until done.

226 To tenderize meat, place in vinegar water for a few minutes.

227 Tenderize meat by adding 2 or 3 tsp. of vinegar to the cooking water.

228 To tenderize steak, rub steak with mixture of vinegar and oil. Allow to stand two hours.

229 To tenderize steak, brush it on both sides with lime juice, a few hours before the steak is cooked.

230 Add a little strong tea to roasts and stews. It acts as a meat tenderizer and reduces cooking time.

231 Tenderize a tough piece of pot roast with tomatoes. Add the tomatoes to the usual vegetables and seasonings and the acid in the tomatoes will act as tenderizer.

232 Buy cheaper cuts of meat and tenderize with inexpensive wine for a gourmet flavor.

233 Let boiled meat go cold in its own broth if you want it to be tender when cold.

234 Beef liver will be tender if soaked in milk. Refrigerate for about two hours then bread and sauté.

235 Instead of greasing your skillet with oil, sprinkle it with salt lightly and hamburgers will fry in their own juices.

236 To stretch ground beef, mix 1½ cups of poultry dressing with one pound of ground beef. It adds flavor to meat loaf or hamburgers.

237 To make same-size hamburgers, use an ice cream scoop to measure out ground beef.

FOOD

FOOD

238 You can decrease the cooking time for hamburgers by making several holes in the centre of each patty.

239 Brown meatballs uniformly and with less mess by doing them on a cookie sheet in a 425°F oven.

240 Use soybeans instead of hamburger for making meatloaf.

241 If meatloaf is placed on a slice of bacon while baking, it won't stick to the pan.

242 Try making meatloaf in muffin tins. It cooks more quickly and looks better.

243 The trick to cutting meat for Chinese dishes is to partially freeze the meat (or partially thaw frozen meat) and then slice it thinly across the grain.

244 To make smooth gravy add the flour to the water in a jar, shake well and pour into the hot liquid to thicken — if you add water to flour it makes lumps.

245 To speed up gravy making, add a bit of club soda to the roasting pan. The browned bits stuck to the bottom of the pan will loosen more quickly.

246 When making a beef stew or gravy, add one tbsp. blackstrap molasses for color and flavor.

247 If the gravy gives out before the roast does, don't use expensive gravy mixes. Instead, use instant beef or chicken bouillon to stretch beef, chicken and turkey gravy. Add a teaspoon or two of the bouillon to a tumbler of water; add flour or cornstarch then mix with a fork and add what's left of the gravy.

248 Cutting your own chicken pieces and chops from whole fryers and loins will easily save 30 to 50 per cent on your meat bill.

249 Defrost chicken by soaking in heavily salted cold water. The meat will be white and flavorful.

250 To make baked chicken easier and tastier, brush chicken pieces with mayonnaise, then coat with crushed, seasoned cracker crumbs and bake. The mayonnaise provides an excellent base and the crumbs stick better.

251 When stuffing a large turkey, line the cavity with cheesecloth, then stuff it. After the turkey is cooked, the stuffing is easy to get out and nothing is left clinging to the bones.

252 Use dental floss to truss turkey or chicken.

253 There's no need to sew up a turkey or chicken after stuffing with dressing. Just insert a heel of bread to close the gap.

254 Save one-third the baking time, by placing chicken or turkey in a well-oiled brown paper bag. Seal end of bag with staples and bake in 400°F oven.

255 Baste turkey with a mixture of two cups water and ¼ cup honey.

256 Don't throw away chicken and turkey livers, hearts and gizzards. Simmer them in water, then cut up. Place water and cut up pieces in blender. Blend and add to gravy.

257 For easier carving, cover a roast or turkey with tinfoil and let stand for about 30 minutes after cooking.

FOOD

FOOD

258 To enable you to have slow-cooking porridge oats in the morning, measure oats into a thermos flask the evening before. Pour on appropriate amount of boiling water and put on lid. Porridge is hot and ready to eat for breakfast.

259 Buy plain cereals rather than the 'with fruit and nuts' variety. Add a handful of raisins, dried chopped apple, prunes, apricots, walnut chips, etc. to make a less costly mixture.

260 To keep dumplings light, prick them open when first taken from the kettle.

261 For light pancakes and waffles, replace the liquid in the batter with club soda.

262 Crêpes can be made ahead of time, frozen in meal-size amounts and reheated in the microwave.

263 If you have pancakes left over, line each with wax paper so they don't stick, place in plastic bag and freeze. When needed, pop into toaster.

264 If you have leftover eggnog, substitute it for the milk called for in plain muffin recipes. It's also good in pancakes.

265 You won't need to invest in a lot of muffin tins if you arrange sealer bands on a cookie sheet then place paper muffin cups in each band.

266 When making cupcakes or muffins, use an ice cream scoop to get the right amount of batter in each muffin cup.

267 If you have trouble getting muffins out the pan, place the bottom of the hot pan on a wet towel for about 30 seconds.

268 If you freeze baker's yeast, it will last indefinitely.

269 To see if old yeast is still good, put a tsp. of yeast in a cup of warm water, add 1 tbsp. sugar. If the mixture foams in ten minutes the yeast is still good for baking.

270 Store an opened bag of flour in an air-tight container or plastic bag to maintain moisture content.

271 Whole-wheat flour stays fresh in a freezer bag in the freezer.

272 When baking buns or bread, place rising dough in oven with light on — temperature is perfect and area is free of drafts.

273 Roll biscuit dough thin then fold it before cutting. This makes biscuits flaky in the center and they will also split open easily for buttering

274 Cut fresh bread with a hot knife.

275 Warm hot dog buns in top of double boiler, while wieners cook in the bottom.

276 Stale rolls can be revived if you spray them lightly with cold water, place in a paper bag or wrap in foil and warm in a 375°F oven for about five minutes.

277 Reheat stale buns and rolls by placing them in a wet brown paper bag and putting it in the oven at 350°F for seven to ten minutes.

278 Don't throw away a stale loaf of bread. Wrap it in a damp cloth for about a minute, then place in preheated 350°F oven for about 20 minutes. Serve warm.

279 Save all leftover bread trimmings and crusts. Put them in a plastic bag and freeze. When you have accumulated enough, use for making bread crumbs, croûtons or stuffings.

FOOD

FOOD

280 Save all dry bread, toast, raisin and fruit breads, stale cakes, etc., in freezer to use when making bread pudding.

281 To freshen dry bread, rolls or doughnuts, place in a covered casserole and place casserole in pan of hot water. Heat thoroughly in the oven.

282 Make your own croûtons. Butter both sides of two or three slices of bread, season as desired and cut into small cubes. Set cubes on cookie sheet and heat them in a 375°F oven for about 15 minutes or until lightly browned.

283 If you run out of bread crumbs, you can use dry cereals by putting them through a blender or food processor.

284 To make bread crumbs, place pieces ⊔i dry bread into a plastic bag and roll with a rolling pin.

285 Make up bread crumbs ahead of time and store for months in plastic bag or container in the freezer.

286 To deter mold, wash your bread box with a mixture of two tbsp. vinegar to a quart of water.

287 You can easily determine whether you need a fresh supply of baking powder by pouring ¼ cup of hot tap water over ½ tsp. of baking powder. If the mixture doesn't bubble actively, it's too old.

288 Keep crackers in the sugar canister to keep sugar from caking.

289 To store brown sugar, wrap it in a plastic bag and place in a coffee can which has a snap-on lid.

290 Brown sugar will keep soft if stored in the freezer.

291 Soften brown sugar by freezing it. It will be soft when thawed.

292 To moisten brown sugar which has hardened, place apple slices in a container with the sugar and cover tightly.

293 Brown sugar can be softened by enclosing a slice of bread in the bag. It will be soft in approximately a day.

294 To soften hard brown sugar, place in sealed container with a couple of marshmallows.

295 One cup of white sugar and two tbsp. molasses make one cup of brown sugar.

296 For a brown sugar substitute, mix together ½ cup white sugar, ½ tsp. maple flavoring and ½ tsp. molasses.

297 When melting chocolate in the microwave or double boiler, line bowl or pot with waxed paper. Chocolate is easy to pour and easy to scrape off the paper. None is wasted.

298 If you do not have any squares of chocolate for baking, substitute 45 mL cocoa plus 10 mL shortening for each square. It's just as good and so much cheaper.

299 When making cookies, add one tsp. of jam or jelly. The cookies will have a better taste and will stay moist longer.

300 To make cakes, cookies, pancakes and waffles especially moist, add two tbsp. honey to the batter.

301 Always store coconut in airtight containers or sealed plastic bags to prevent drying out.

302 For tinted coconut, add a few drops of food coloring to a small amount of water. Pour over flaked or shredded coconut in a jar. Cover and shake until thoroughly colored.

FOOD

FOOD

303 One tsp. of cornstarch will improve texture and flavor of fudge.

304 A little flour added to icing sugar makes it go a lot further.

305 Marshmallows will not dry out if stored in the freezer. Cut up with scissors when you want to use them.

306 When cutting marshmallows or gumdrops, dip scissors in hot water.

307 Crushed cornflakes can be used as a substitute for pecans.

308 Coarse bran may be used in place of chopped nuts when making chocolate brownies.

309 Keep nuts, especially Brazil nuts, in the freezer. They will come out of the shell easier and won't break up.

310 Walnuts which have an 'old' taste can be improved in flavor by pouring boiling water over them, then spreading in a shallow pan and heating in the oven. Stir often to prevent burning.

311 Keep peanut butter fresh by storing the jar upside down.

312 When you double a recipe, just use the original amount of salt.

313 For a quick and inexpensive ice cream sauce, melt one Fudgesicle for two servings.

314 When measuring molasses, honey and other syrups. Dust the cup with flour or oil the syrup will come out easier.

315 A small two-inch paintbrush will last longer and stay more pliable than a pastry brush.

316 Rinse your measuring cup with oil, then rinse in hot water, before measuring sticky liquids. They will pour easily.

317 To make cake flour, sift together two tbsp. cornstarch to one cup of all-purpose flour.

318 Batter: To avoid lumps add a pinch of salt to the flour before adding liquid ingredients.

319 To color sugar for decorating cakes, cookies, etc., put one or two drops of food coloring in a small plastic bag. Add one or two tsp. of white sugar and tie top of bag securely. Work sugar and coloring together with fingers until sugar is evenly colored.

320 When making quick breads, cakes and cookies, cut sugar by one-third to one-half. Bring out sweetness by using vanilla extract.

321 Creaming shortening and sugar is easier if a few drops of water are sprinkled on top of the mixture.

322 When making a cake, always add two tbsp. boiling water to the butter and sugar mixture. This makes a fine-textured cake.

323 When making a cake, or any recipe that calls for mixing dry ingredients together then adding them at a later point, put them all in a paper bag or plastic bag and shake to mix. You have no separate bowl to clean and no fuss or muss either.

324 If batter always rises up the mixer beaters, spray the beaters with a nonstick vegetable oil spray before using.

325 Roll raisins or dried fruit in flour before stirring them into cake batter to prevent them from sinking to the bottom.

FOOD

FOOD

326 To keep raisins from sinking to the bottom of your cake, toss in butter or heat in oven for a moment before stirring into batter.

327 Leave cloves out of spice cake if you plan to freeze it. Cloves get stronger in cold storage.

328 Keep a mixture of equal parts flour and shortening at room temperature. Use to grease cake pans.

329 Line cake pans with margarine wrappers instead of wax paper.

330 Use the parchment from margarine and butter wrappers to grease cake and cookie pans.

331 Quick-cool angel food cake by inverting pan over a tray of ice cubes.

332 Sprinkle cake plate with granulated sugar to prevent cake from sticking when serving.

333 To keep icing from running off a cake, dust the cake with powdered sugar before icing.

334 When you're ready to frost the cupcakes you've made to pack in lunches, don't frost the tops. Slit the cupcakes in half, frost the centres and put back together. This way, the frosting won't stick to the sandwich bags.

335 Use a clean squeeze-type ketchup or mustard container for decorating cakes.

336 Make a handy, disposable paper funnel for icing cakes by snipping off a corner of an envelope.

337 A slice of apple or potato under the cake plate dome will keep cake fresh.

338 When you are slicing only a few pieces from a freshly-baked cake, take the slices from the centre then slide the two halves together. The cake will stay fresh longer.

339 Attach a slice of bread, with toothpicks, to cut edge of a cake. This will keep cake fresh until it is cut again.

340 Before placing a tube cake in a cake server, put a glass or plastic bottle with water in the centre of the cake. This will keep the cake extra moist for a week or longer.

341 Slice leftover cake, wrap individual pieces and freeze. Put in school or work lunches and the cake will be thawed by noon.

342 Don't throw away stale cake — you can make a fine dessert with it. Soak pieces of the cake in rum, then mix into a thick vanilla pudding and chill. Cover with whipped cream or decorate with slivered almonds or serve with fruit syrup.

343 If you're running low on flour, substitute fine bread crumbs, plain or toasted, for all or part of the flour in cookies.

344 Cookie dough that is to be rolled is much easier to handle after it has been chilled 10 to 30 minutes. This keeps the dough from sticking, even though it may be soft.

345 Sliced cookies from refrigerator dough will always be perfectly shaped if you freeze the dough in small frozen juice cans or plastic wrap cartons.

346 When rolling out dough on wax paper, aluminum foil or plastic wrap, wet the surface of the counter before smoothing the paper down and the water will keep the paper in place.

FOOD

FOOD

347 Use a melon ball scoop or a small ice cream scoop to drop cookie dough on baking sheets. It saves time and cookies are a uniform size.

348 Use the liners from cereal boxes to line cookie tins.

349 Don't ruin a pan of cookies. Always bake one cookie first, even when using a familiar recipe, because the moisture content of flour can vary greatly.

350 When sprinkling sugar on cookies, use a salt shaker or empty spice container.

351 Save meat trays and freeze muffins, cookies, portions or slices of cake on them. They can be stacked neatly in the freezer without crushing or crumbling.

352 For better pie crusts, make certain all ingredients are cold and do not overwork the dough. Cover the dough and refrigerate before rolling out.

353 To roll out pastry, use two squares of wax paper which have been lightly floured. Roll out the pie crust dough between these sheets. When the pie crust is the correct size, peel off the top sheet of wax paper; invert over the pie plate and peel off the bottom layer of paper.

354 Keep a small plastic bag handy while making pie crust, kneading bread or mixing meat loaf. Use it to slip your hand into if you have to answer the phone, doorbell or open the refrigerator or cupboard door.

355 Pastry will be flakier if you include one tbsp. orange or lemon juice as part of the liquid.

356 To prevent a pie shell from blistering, place a few slices of bread in it before baking. Remove bread during the last few minutes of baking time. The bread can be used for croûtons in soup.

357 To prevent the bottom pie crust from becoming soggy, grease pie plate with butter before putting in dough. The crust will be soft and flaky.

358 Sprinkle sugar on pie crust before adding cream filling. This will prevent a soggy crust.

359 Minute Tapioca is excellent for thickening fruit pies — two tbsp. for a small pie and three tbsp. for a larger, deeper fruit pie.

360 Short pieces of drinking straws inserted into the centre of a pie will stop the juices from escaping or running over in your oven.

361 Place a layer of marshmallows in the bottom of pumpkin pie. The marshmallows will rise to the top, forming a fluffy topping.

362 Meringue will not shrink if spread on pie so that the meringue touches all edges of the pie crust.

363 Always bake a two-crust pie on the bottom shelf of the oven. This will bake the bottom thoroughly and the pie will brown lightly on top.

364 For fluffy meringue, add ¼ tsp. white vinegar to three egg whites.

365 To keep the edge of a pie crust from getting too brown or burnt, cut out the centre of a foil pan to the exact size of the pie that you are baking and place it over the pie just as soon as it begins to darken.

366 To remove chiffon pie from pie plate with graham cracker crust intact, dip pan in warm water for a few seconds.

367 Use a buttered knife to slice soft pies easily.

FOOD

FOOD

368 For a better pop, place popcorn kernels in cold water for five minutes before popping.

369 Store popping corn in the freezer and use it directly from the freezer. You will get puffier, larger kernels of popcorn and more of the kernels will pop.

370 Keep popping corn in the refrigerator and you will get fewer unpopped kernels.

371 Preheat the hot-air popcorn popper and you will have very few unpopped kernels and fluffier popcorn.

372 Instead of buying baby food, purchase frozen vegetables and purée them in your food processor. Spoon into ice cube trays and freeze. Wrap in individual servings for future use. The same process can be followed for daily leftovers of meats and vegetables.

373 Make your own baby food and freeze it in disposable bottle liners. Measure the food into the sac inside the bottle, twist-tie it and slip it out the bottom of the bottle. Increase amounts of food in the sac as baby's appetite increases. It's a sanitary way of freezing baby food and it doesn't take on any freezer odors. To use, just dip sac in warm water, slide food out and heat.

374 If you plan to eat in restaurants while travelling, make lunch your main meal of the day. Many places charge more for the same meal at night.

LAUNDRY

375 Soak new, brightly colored garments in cold, salty water before laundering. The colors will stay brighter.

376 When washing colored or printed material for the first time, add one tsp. Epsom salts to one gallon of water. The material will neither fade nor run.

377 Soaking blue jeans in ½ cup vinegar and two quarts water for one hour before the first washing helps prevent them from fading.

378 When washing blue jeans, wash in cold water, put in dryer for 10 minutes or so, then fold on a wooden clothes hanger and continue to dry.

379 Always turn corduroy pants inside out before washing. This will keep them lint free and they will also last longer.

380 Pin socks in pairs before washing them and you won't waste time trying to match them up.

381 Rub a sticky zipper with a lead pencil.

382 Rub beeswax inside and outside your zippers on boots, purses, jackets, etc. to keep them running smoothly and quietly. This also removes dust and grime.

LAUNDRY

383 To save on drycleaning bills, wash your wool blankets in a mild dishwasher soap or Zero on a gentle cycle. Dry on air fluff.

384 Silk garments must be hand washed. Use cool water with Lux or Zero soap. When rinsing, add a bit of lanolin to restore and protect the material. Drip dry and press, using a soft cloth.

385 Club soda is a great stain remover for clothing.

386 To make your own spot remover, combine two parts water with one part rubbing alcohol.

387 Glass cleaner is a good spot remover. If you get a spot on a dress, for example, place a tissue on your hand under the spot. Give the spot a spray of glass cleaner and rub gently, using another tissue on top to make the spot disappear. Reapply if necessary.

388 To make your own prewash spray combine ⅓ cup each of water, liquid detergent and ammonia. Mix, then store in a spray bottle. This is excellent to spray on collars, spots and stains.

389 Use vinegar to remove perspiration, grass and slight scorch stains from clothing.

390 To remove stains, soak garment in baking soda and water for several hours, then wash as usual.

391 Dissolve your soap flakes thoroughly in water before putting into washing machine. This will eliminate powdery buildups on clothes and extra washings.

392 To use up slivers of soap, put them in a white sock, tie a knot in the sock and toss into the washing machine. This will keep your socks whiter and save money because you add less detergent.

393 Always measure any detergent used with appropriate scoops. This prevents using an excessive amount.

394 If you accidentally put too much soap in the washer, pour two tbsp. vinegar or a capful of fabric softener into the machine.

395 To make certain that clothes receive a thorough rinsing, add one cup white vinegar to the rinse cycle. This will help dissolve the alkalines in soaps and detergents, plus it will give you soft, sweet-smelling clothes.

396 When washing clothes, use cold water for the rinse cycle. Clothes will retain their shape and color better.

397 Clean your washing machine by occasionally running through the wash cycle, using warm water and vinegar. Do not put clothes in for this.

398 For a whiter wash, add ¼ cup dishwasher detergent to your load of white wash.

399 Dishwasher detergent can be used to whiten sweat socks and cottons. Just add to regular washload.

400 Instead of bleach, use about three tbsp. peroxide in your wash.

401 White socks can be white again if you soak them in boiling water to which a slice of lemon has been added. Wash as usual.

402 To bleach handkerchiefs, soak ½ hour in sour milk and wash as usual.

403 To whiten lace, wash in sour milk.

LAUNDRY

LAUNDRY

404 For removal of various food stains or ground-in dirt, grass stains, etc., on clothing use Sunlight Dish Soap. Wet the spot, put dish soap on spot, rub well, then wash as normal in the washing machine.

405 To get stains out of white T-shirts or shirts (especially tomato stains) wet stains with water and sprinkle with Comet cleaner, wait for 15 minutes, rinse. Works well.

406 To remove fresh blood stains, soak garment in cold water for 24 hours. Change water several times.

407 To remove blood stains, cover stains with a paste of meat tenderizer and cold water, let stand 15-30 minutes, then sponge with cool water.

408 To remove blood stains, dab with hydrogen peroxide. It will fizz up and the stain will disappear.

409 To remove blood stains from clothing, sponge the stain with three-percent hydrogen peroxide. Let soak for a few seconds, rub, then launder as usual.

410 When fruit juice is spilled on a tablecloth or clothing, boil a kettle full of water and pour full kettle directly over the stain. The stain will be removed immediately.

411 Grass stains on clothing are easy to remove if rubbed with blackboard chalk before washing,

412 Rub toothpaste on grass stains, before laundering, for easy removal.

413 To remove grass stains from children's clothing and white shoes, just rub the stain well with molasses, leave overnight, then wash with soap (not detergent.) The stains will disappear like magic.

414 Most grass stains can be removed with methyl alcohol. (REMEMBER: Test colors first to see if they are affected.) If a stain remains on white material, use a mild solution of sodium perborate, chlorine bleach or hydrogen peroxide.

415 Grease and oil stains may be removed from fabric by first rubbing lard on the spots, then wash with liquid detergent. Repeat if necessary.

416 Pour a few drops of Pine Sol in your wash water to remove grease or oil from clothes.

417 Put ¼ cup Spic and Span in your wash water for each tub of clothes to help remove stains and grease.

418 To remove grease and dirt spots, put cornstarch on grease spots and rub in. Brush off the cornstarch.

419 Greasy work clothes will wash easily if you add a bottle of cola to the detergent.

420 To remove grease or lipstick stains, pour Mr. Clean on the stain, rub in and wash normally.

421 To remove lipstick from linen napkins, dab on a little petroleum jelly, then wash.

422 To remove grease from suede, sponge with a cloth dipped in vinegar or club soda. Restore the suede by brushing with a suede brush.

423 Place clothing, which has gum stuck to it, in the freezer for a couple of hours. Remove from freezer and crumble off gum.

424 To remove ink from clothing, use a dab of toothpaste.

425 Ink stains on clothes disappear when hairspray is used on them prior to washing the article as usual.

426 To remove ink from any material, place a slice of raw tomato on the ink spot. It will soak up the ink and then you can wash the material as usual.

427 To remove ballpoint pen from dolls, use a lemon juice and salt mixture on the ink and leave in the sun for a few hours. Wipe clean.

428 Wet iodine stains with water, then put baking soda on thickly and let stand.

429 To remove ring around the collar, rub shampoo on the ring and wash in the usual manner.

LAUNDRY

LAUNDRY

430 For ring around the collar use a mixture of ⅓ cup Palmolive dish soap, ⅓ cup ammonia and ⅓ cup water. Place mixture in a squeeze bottle and rub on with an old toothbrush.

431 Buy a large bottle of liquid starch concentrate and mix one-part starch to one-part water and pour into a spray bottle to make your own spray starch. A light spray of starch helps prevent ring around the collar and protects against various stains.

432 To remove rust marks from clothing, squeeze lemon juice on the spots, pat with salt and hang the garment in the sun to dry.

433 To remove tar from clothing, rub tar with lots of butter and scrub until the tar is removed. Use Spray & Wash or similar product to remove the butter.

434 To get rid of tea stains from a tablecloth, dab with glycerine, leave overnight and then wash in normal manner.

435 To remove candle wax, melt wax between blotters or rub with ice cubes and scrape off. Wax dye stains can be removed with alcohol or bleach in water.

436 Place water-stained fabric (curtains for example) in salted water and soak until the stain disappears.

437 To remove red wine from a tablecloth, moisten spot, apply salt, let stand a moment or two and wash thoroughly as usual.

438 If colors run when clothes are washed, rub Palmolive liquid detergent into the stained area. Soak clothing in cold water. Reapply detergent to area and gently rub with a toothbrush. Then let the clothing sit, for approximately 2 hours to let the detergent soak into the fabric. Then rewash clothing in the normal fashion.

439 To remove smoke odor from clothing, fill the bathtub with hot water to which a cup or two of vinegar has been added. Hang articles of smoky clothing in the bathroom overnight, keeping the door closed. The vinegar will neutralize the smoke odor.

440 Put a drop of Nilodor in each load of laundry to eliminate all odors.

441 To remove mildew from shower curtains, wash in a mixture of ½ cup bleach, one gallon water and ½ cup detergent.

442 When washing plastic curtains or tablecloths, add one cup vinegar to the rinse water. The plastic will dry soft and pliable thus prolonging the life of the item.

443 To soften stiff plastic pants and prolong their use, put them in a dryer wih a load of towels.

444 To keep your sheer curtains wrinkle free, add a package of unflavored gelatin, which has been dissolved in a cup of boiling water, to the final rinse.

445 When washing lace or sheer curtains, add 1 cup of Epsom salts to the last rinse. The Epsom salts give the curtains body and they also last longer.

446 Throw a dry bath towel into the dryer when drying a load. Laundry will dry a lot quicker, therefore saving power and wear on the dryer.

447 Dilute liquid fabric softener before adding it to the wash, otherwise it can cause greasy looking stains on fabrics.

448 If you use fabric softener sheets, use them twice then store in a jar with liquid fabric softener. When drying a load of clothes, pull out a sheet, squeeze out the excess solution and toss in the dryer.

LAUNDRY

LAUNDRY

449 When washing drapes and wanting that perfect pleated effect, press, hang, open and run fingers down each individual pleat, while holding together at the bottom. Wrap a tie around the centre and about two-thirds of the way down. Leave for 24 hours.

450 Use rubbing alcohol to remove ballpoint pen marks on clothing and upholstery.

451 If your slipcovers are washable, place back on your furniture while still damp. They will fit better and won't require ironing because as they finish drying they conform to the shape of the furniture and stretch out the wrinkles.

452 Rubbing cornmeal into a grease stain on upholstery and vacuuming it the next day will lift out the mark.

453 Spruce up old stuffed nonwashable toys by placing in a bag with baking soda. Shake and brush off.

454 Clean white kid gloves with flour. Just rub it into the dirt and brush it away.

455 To clean silk flowers, put flowers in a plastic bag with a couple tablespoons of salt. Shake vigorously while holding stems and bag shut. The dust will cling to the salt and the flowers will look like new.

456 Dry lingerie on a clothes line or place on a clothers hanger to dry. Heat from the dryer will ruin the elastic.

457 Use half of a fabric-softening sheet for a regular-size load of laundry in the dryer. It is as effective as a full sheet.

458 Mix two cups fabric softener with two cups water and store in covered plastic container. Dip an old facecloth in the solution and use instead of fabric softener sheet.

459 Lint from the dryer and from the washing machine, along with other garbage collected in the laundry area, can easily be placed in the empty soap box. This saves space in the garbage and also saves on garbage bags.

460 To remove burrs from sweaters or slacks, use disposable razors.

461 For best results when hand washing sweaters, put a capful of hair cream rinse in the final rinse.

462 Wool is weak when wet. Do not pull, wring or rub wet wool garments. Lay the garment on a towel, roll it up and gently squeeze.

463 Shrunken woollens may loosen and stretch if soaked in a hair cream rinse.

464 To unshrink woollens, dissolve one oz. Borax in one tsp. hot water and add to one gallon warm water. Immerse garment, pull gently into shape and rinse in one gallon warm water to which two tbsp. vinegar have been added.

465 To tighten stretched sweater cuffs, dip in hot water and dry with a hairdryer.

466 Turn acrylic sweaters inside out when washing them to avoid getting fuzz balls on them.

467 To avoid ironing clothes, take them out of the dryer as soon as it stops and fold them.

468 If you can't iron damp clothes right away, put them in a plastic bag and place in the freezer. They will be easier to iron and there's no danger of mildew.

469 To keep delicate fabrics from becoming shiny when ironing, cover the material with a sheet of tissue paper. Make certain the iron isn't too hot.

LAUNDRY

LAUNDRY

470 An iron heats faster than it cools. Therefore, iron fabrics which need a cool temperature setting first, then iron fabrics which require higher temperatures.

471 Pressing pleats in a skirt will take less time if bobby pins are used to hold them in place. They may be left in position while pressing all but the hem and then removed to complete the job.

472 After letting down a hem, rub vinegar on the old mark. Press with a hot iron — the old hem mark disappears and so does the vinegar.

473 Place a sheet of aluminum foil under your ironing board cover. It will hold the heat longer.

474 Scorch marks may be removed by using a cloth dampened with vinegar. Place it over the scorched area and apply a warm iron.

475 To treat scorch marks on cotton, press with a warm iron on a cloth dipped in peroxide.

476 Stop your iron from sticking by running it back and forth, while hot, over a piece of paper on which salt has been sprinkled.

477 When your iron is off and unplugged, use pipecleaners dipped in sudsy water to clean out the steam holes.

478 Starch stuck to the bottom of an iron can be removed by rubbing a damp cloth sprinkled with dry baking soda over the bottom plate of the iron.

479 Clean a dirty iron bottom with a dampened SOS pad. Then, warm the iron and run over a piece of wax paper to restore the shiny finish.

480 Use elastic thread to sew buttons on coats or other heavy garments. They will stay on long and be easier to use.

481 Before you wear a new garment (or even on old ones) touch the centre of each button, front and back, with clear nail polish. This will seal the threads and the buttons will stay on much longer.

482 Find buttons easily. Sort them by size or color in the compartments of an egg carton.

483 When sewing on a button, especially a large one, place a pin under the thread at the back of the button. When finished pull out the pin. The button has room to move and will last longer.

484 Sew buttons on children's clothing with dental floss — it's much stronger than thread.

485 When removing buttons from a discarded item, sew them together before storing with your spares. It will save you the time of having to match buttons later.

486 Button popped off? For a quick fix, reattach it with the wire from a twist tie.

487 Stop tangled thread. For a single thread, knot and cut from spool last; and for double thread, knot each end separately.

488 Wet your finger before slipping on your sewing thimble. The suction will keep the thimble from slipping off.

489 Always place a used desk blotter under your sewing machine needle when oiling the machine to keep from soiling thread and material.

490 To sharpen your sewing machine needle, stitch through a piece of fine sandpaper.

LAUNDRY

LAUNDRY

491 When elastic that is sewed on a garment becomes worn or stretched, just baste cord elastic through the worn elastic. Pull it up and knot.

492 When patching the knees of your gardening jeans, leave the top of each patch open like a pocket so that you can slip in pieces of foam rubber for knee pads. They will make kneeling more comfortable.

493 Save old drapery draw cord and use the good portions for replacement drawstrings in rugby pants and pyjamas. Just thread through the waistband, using a large safety pin, and make a knot in each end to hold.

494 Discarded neckties make interesting women's belts when three are braided together. Single ties may be opened to serve as a neck kerchief on a dress or sweater.

495 Men's cotton-blend shirts make good coveralls or aprons. Just cut away the collar, shorten the sleeves (if long sleeved) and finish the neckline with bias tape.

496 When the feet on men's socks wear out, cut them off at the ankle. Stitch along the bottom and use as children's socks.

497 Using your old quilted housecoat for the inside of a baby quilt makes use of a useless housecoat and is an inexpensive light filling for the quilt.

498 To recycle wrinkled ribbon, run through a warm curling iron.

499 When a bedsheet begins to show wear, cut the sheet in half across, bring the unhemmed top and bottom ends together and sew them together. Hem the centre ends with one narrow hem and one wider hem. The worn ends will be on the top and bottom of the sheet, making the sheet last a few years longer.

500 Recyle old bedsheets by cutting them into pillowcases.

501 Cotton sheets can be recycled into pillowcases.

502 Old flannel sheets can be used to make a child's nightgown or pyjamas.

503 To wear sheets evenly, place a safety pin in the bottom end of your sheet. After every wash, place the safety pin to the other end of the sheet and make your bed with that end to the bottom.

504 Use scrap material or old sheets, towels etc. to make gift bags. Cut material into the size you need, sew a one-inch seam for the drawstring and sew bag together.

505 Use old blankets instead of batting when making quilts.

506 Trim old tablecloths into a number of napkins.

507 Turn two old bath towels into a duvet cover for your cat's bed. Simply sew together on three sides like a pillow slip and slide in a scrap piece of fibreglass insulation batting, wrapped in a plastic drycleaner's bag. The cover is easy to slide off for laundering.

508 Baby's receiving blankets can be sewn together to make a special quilt.

509 Key chains sewed into the collars of children's coats and jackets provide strong hangers.

LAUNDRY

LAUNDRY

510 When small children have difficulty zipping their jackets, make it easier for them by attaching a key ring to the zipper pull.

511 To make a child's 'emergency throw-away apron,' take a plastic shopping bag with hand holes at the top and cut down one side and across the bottom. Open and use as an apron by pinning at the back.

512 To remove scuff marks from white shoes, rub with dressmaker's chalk and polish.

513 Give suede shoes a new look by wiping with a sponge moistened in cool black coffee.

514 A cloth dampened with vinegar will remove grease stains on suede shoes.

515 Add extra shine to your shoes by putting a couple drops of lemon juice on them when polishing.

516 Furniture polish is an excellent substitute for shoe polish. Spray an even coat on the shoes, wipe dry and buff to a shine.

517 Polish your shoes well once, then when they look dull wipe them with a soft cloth dampened with baby oil.

518 Paint heels of shoes with clear nail polish to prevent scuffing the finish.

519 Spray the insides of new running shoes with spray starch and let dry overnight. The starch will keep the insides clean and keep the runners fresher for longer.

520 After washing running shoes, spray with spray starch. This will help resist soil.

521 To dry the inside of children's winter boots or summer rubbers quickly, put the hose of the vacuum cleaner into the boot and turn on the blower.

522 If your shoelaces are always coming undone, dampen with a spray of water before tying.

523 To renew shoelaces which have lost their plastic tips, dip the ends in nail polish.

524 To make children's shoelaces last longer, stitch up and down new laces with the sewing machine before putting in shoes.

525 If sandals pinch, dab the inside with rubbing alcohol and wear them immediately. The leather strap will ease a bit over the tight spot.

526 Kerosene will soften boots and shoes which have become hardened by water.

527 Erase 'wet' rings on smooth leather boots by brushing spots with a mixture of equal parts vinegar and cold water.

528 To remove salt from boots, make a solution of two parts water, one part white vinegar. Pour into a spray bottle and use on boots as needed.

GROOMING

529 Create your own spa, add one cup of natural, no additive Sifto pickling salt to your next bath. Relax in the warm salt water.

530 Here's an inexpensive bath oil: use peanut oil, safflower oil or sunflower oil in a hot tub of water. Put your favorite herbs, lavender, basil or rose petals in a little bag and let the water run over it. You get the oil and the sweet scent for little cost.

531 To save on bubble bath, make your own by placing your soap slivers into a terry drawstring bag. Dangle bag from the tap at bath time, allowing the water to run over and through it.

532 If you run an inch of cold water in the bathtub before adding hot water, your bathroom will be free of steam.

533 To save on hand soap, stock up when it's on sale, then unwrap each bar before storing. This allows the bars to dry out and become harder, which makes them last longer when used.

534 To make your own liquid hand soap, you need one (3.5 ounce) bar of soap (choose soap which contains moisturizing cream) and three cups of water. Grate soap, add water and microwave on high until well dissolved. Stir every two minutes. Cool and pour into a dispenser.

535 To use up small pieces of soap, soften in the microwave for a few seconds on a piece of plastic wrap. Then add to your new bar.

536 Bits and pieces of hand soap can be used up by putting into a toe of a nylon stocking and tied.

537 After washing and drying your hands, make a cup of one hand and pour in some vinegar. Carefully coat both hands as you would with hand cream. You will have soft hands.

538 Rub your hands with vinegar to get rid of food odors such as fish, garlic and onion.

539 Vinegar will remove fruit and vegetable stains from hands.

540 To get the onion smell out of your hands, rub them with a little dry mustard.

541 Onion on Hands: To remove onion odor from hands rub each finger vigorously with celery salt before washing.

542 To remove paint smells from your hands, use water and lemon juice.

543 Dip hands in lemon juice to whiten fingernail tips.

544 Before going to work in your garden, rub your nails over a bar of soap. This will prevent the dirt from getting your nails.

545 Lather soap in your hands and add ½ tsp. sugar to the lather to remove gardening stains from your hands.

546 To save money on special soap, use laundry detergent as a hand cleaner for greasy, oily hands.

547 Before starting to clean your oven, use Lustre Sheen cream hand cleaner with lanolin underneath your fingernails. Also coat your hands lightly. Your hands will come clean easily after the job is done.

548 If you're bothered by hangnails, place Vitamin E around the cuticles.

549 Baby oil does the same job as cleansing creams but at less than half the price.

GROOMING

GROOMING

550 To prepare cleansing cream, place ¼ cup honey, 1 tbsp. liquid soap, ½ cup glycerin in a screw-top jar, cover and shake well. Makes about ¾ cup cleansing cream.

551 To make a facial mask for oily skin, combine 2 tbsp. finely ground oatmeal and 2 tbsp. honey. Apply mixture to skin, leave on for 15 minutes. Wash off with warm water.

552 A good facial mask for oily skin, apply plain buttermilk on the skin, leave on for 15 minutes. Wash off with warm water.

553 To save on costly facials here are two inexpensive homemade treatments. For normal to oily skin: one cup yogurt, one tsp. fresh lemon juice, one tsp. fresh orange juice and one tsp. carrot juice. Blend ingredients and apply to face, leaving on 10-15 minutes. Rinse with tepid water. For dry skin: ¼ mashed avocado, ½ mashed banana, two tbsp. plain yogurt and one tsp. wheat-germ oil. Combine and use as directed above.

554 Use solid canned shortening as a makeup remover.

555 Blemishes will fade if you dab a little lemon juice on them.

556 Lemon rubbed on the skin will keep it white.

557 At the end of the day, lemon slices rubbed on the feet will freshen them

558 Dead skin will peel off elbows, knees, feet and face which has been massaged with Miracle Whip Salad Dressing.

559 For an inexpensive shampoo, mix ½ cup vinegar, ½ cup dish detergent, ¼ cup water and two tsps. mayonnaise.

560 To stretch shampoo, mix one pouch of unflavored Knox gelatin into one cup of warm water. Shake well. Pour your shampoo into a quart jar and add gelatin mixture.

561 Make every drop of shampoo count. To use those last drops in the bottle, add a little water, shake the bottle and use. This works for hair conditioner as well.

562 Put an end to shampoo waste by filling a clean plastic pump bottle with shampoo. A few pumps will deliver the desired amount of shampoo and there will be no more spills.

563 To add lustre to brunette or red hair, after shampooing rinse with black coffee, followed by clear water.

564 A bit of vinegar in the final rinse water will make hair shiny.

565 To prepare a treatment for dry damaged hair, stir together 3 tbsp. honey, 1 tbsp. olive oil for 1 minute, until mixture is smooth. Apply to freshly shampooed hair, let soak in for 10-12 minutes. Rinse off with warm water. This makes enough for 1 application.

566 Do you ever spray hair spray in your face, because you couldn't see the hole clearly? Paint a dot of colored nail polish above the hole and you'll see it everytime — no more wasting hair spray.

567 If your young daughter's hair has a tendency to spring out of rollers, fold strips of wet-strength facial tissue around each strand of hair before rolling on the roller. The curls will dry quickly and will be softer.

GROOMING

GROOMING

568 To remove gum from a child's hair, apply Spray & Wash generously to the gum then rub hair between fingers. Comb the gum out and wash hair.

569 To remove gum from a child's hair, use a little peanut butter and rub until the gum disappears.

570 For an inexpensive homemade deodorant, make a dusting powder of equal parts baking soda, cornstarch and a pinch of ground cloves.

571 Use baking powder as a deodorant. Just pat it on as you would powder.

572 Clean dentures with lemon juice for a fresh-tasting mouth.

573 Soak your dentures in white vinegar overnight. It's an inexpensive and effective way to clean them.

574 TV commercials show toothpaste applied the full-length of the brush. All that is necessary is about ¼ inch on the brush.

575 If you run out of toothpaste, use baking soda.

576 Get the last bit of toothpaste out by placing the tube under hot water before rolling and squeezing it.

577 To get rid of onion breath, chew parsley with vinegar on it.

578 Another way to get rid of onion breath is to drink a cup of strong coffee.

579 Use a little salt in warm water for a mouthwash.

580 Put your dentures in a cup of bleach for about 10 minutes. Rinse thoroughly and your dentures will be sparkling clean.

581 If you use a razor and foam to shave, dry your blades well after use and apply a thin layer of petroleum jelly. Then, with a soft facial tissue, wipe off any excess jelly. This will form a coating over the blades, making them last up to five times longer and ensuring a comfortable shave the next morning.

582 To make your own hand lotion combine four ounces glycerine, two ounces alcohol, one dram gum-tragocanth (chips) and one pint of warm soft water. Mix and let stand 24 hours, shaking often. A favorite perfume could also be added.

583 Make your own suntan oil cheaply by combining ½ cup olive oil and ½ cup cider vinegar.

584 To prepare your own lip balm, in a double boiler, melt together 2 tbsp. beeswax and 1 tbsp. coconut oil. Pour into a container while still hot; it will harden as it cools. This makes about ¼ cup of lip balm.

585 Fill a jar of pressed rose petals (or any sweetly-scented flowers), add as much glycerin as the container will hold and cover tightly. After three weeks or so, pour off the perfume into a perfume bottle.

586 If you're getting tired of your perfume and want to switch for awhile, put your old bottle in the refrigerator. It will not deteriorate and you can go back to it again when you feel like it.

587 Don't throw away perfume that is not "you" — use a few drops in the bathtub or sprinkle a few drops on a lightbulb for a lovely scent when the light is turned on.

588 Store nail polishes in the refrigerator. They will go on more smoothly and last much longer.

GROOMING

GROOMING

589 Grease the threaders on nail polish bottles and the lids won't stick.

590 Brushes and combs will come out like new if you soak them 15-20 minutes in a pot of lukewarm water to which one tbsp. baking soda or a little ammonia has been added.

591 To clean hairbrushes, after hair has been removed, rinse brushes throughly in cold water to which ammonia has been added. Shake and dry.

592 To clean hairbrushes and combs combine ¼ cup bleach, one cup water and two tbsp. baking soda. Put in a jar and let combs and brushes soak in solution for a few hours. The solution can be reused. (CAUTION: This solution will break down protein (hair) and therefore, cannot be used to clean natural fibres such as pig bristle.)

593 Contact lenses lost? Turn out the lights and use a flashlight. The lens will show up when the light falls on it.

594 Use pierced earrings as a brooch on a sweater. That way they serve a dual purpose.

595 Put a piece of chalk in your jewelry box to prevent costume jewelry from tarnishing.

596 To prevent tangled necklaces, hang from cup hooks which have been put into a wooden hanger.

597 Use fishing line to restring necklaces. It's easy to handle and extremely strong.

598 Use empty egg cartons to store jewelry — the bottom for earrings, the lid for necklaces.

599 When a ring gets stuck on your finger due to swelling, place your hand in a bowl of ice water. Soak until the ring slips off.

600 Put a folded fabric softener sheet in a small plastic bag and place in your purse. If static cling strikes while you're out, rub the sheet over slip, pantihose or other items of clothing. A single sheet can be used many times.

FIRST AID

601   For an inexpensive antacid powder, use ½ tsp. baking soda in a glass of water.

602   When a pill sticks in your throat, eat a banana. The soft bulk of the fruit moves the medication along.

603   To get a young child to take distasteful medicine, run an ice cube over his tongue — this temporarily freezes the tastebuds.

604   For a cough remedy try this. Boil a lemon in a cup of water. Remove lemon, cut in half and extract juice. To the juice add ½ cup honey and mix well. Take a teaspoon at a time as needed. Stir well before taking each dose.

605   To get relief from a sore throat, gargle with one tsp. salt in ¾ cup warm water.

606   Putting a dab of honey on the back on your tongue can bring relief from a nagging cough.

607   Use Watkins oil and black pepper on the forehead and sinus area for quick headache relief.

608   Hot coffee burned your tongue? A few grains of sugar sprinkled on the sore spot will undo the misery.

FIRST AID

609 Soothe a minor kitchen burn by rubbing it gently with the cut surface of a raw potato.

610 When cooking and you get a burn from a grease splatter, spray immediately with hairspray. It seals off the air and takes away the sting.

611 Ease a burn from hot grease with vanilla extract.

612 A bit of toothpaste on a small burn is a quick healer.

613 To treat minor burns, keep an aloe vera plant in the kitchen. Break off part of the fleshy leaf and split it open. Apply to the burned area.

614 For burn or sunburn relief, apply cold iced tea. Dip a sponge in the tea and pat gently on the burn every 10-15 minutes until the pain is relieved.

615 Put vinegar on sunburns and they won't blister.

616 For sunburn, mix some salt into ice cold milk. Sponge the sunburn once or twice with this mixture.

617 Put Epsom salts in your bath water to relieve aches and pains.

618 A recipe for stiff muscle rub: Combine 2 cups isopropyl alcohol, 1/2 cup methyl salicylate, 1/8 teaspoon camphor, 1/8 teaspoon menthol. Stir in 1/4 cup mineral oil. Effective, but poisonous. Keep out of the reach of children and mark the container well.

619 To make insect repellent, into 1/2 cup denatured alcohol stir 1 tablespoon camphor, 1 tablespoon calcium chloride. Stir until the camphor is dissolved and rub on exposed skin.

620 To get relief from wasp stings, soak stung area in ice water, to which a little Dettol has been added.

621 If you are stung by a bee, head to the spice rack — ¼ tsp. meat tenderizer added to one or two tsp. water (enough to make a paste) will stop the pain in seconds.

622 To relieve bumble bee stings, mix equal parts of baking soda and vinegar and put on bee stings.

623 Bee sting — Slice an onion and rub the onion on the bee sting to take the sting out.

624 Dab vinegar on mosquito bites to relieve itching.

625 Relief for mosquito bites — moisten a bar of soap, rub on the bite. This will stop the itching and acts as a disinfectant to prevent infection.

626 To relieve itching from mosquito bites, apply a bit of toothpaste.

627 To get rid of hair lice, boil quassia chips (obtained from any herbalist) into a tea. Wash hair with this tea and rinse well.

628 For rashes or chicken pox, make a paste of cornstarch, baby oil and a small amount of water. Pat on the paste to stop the itch.

629 Sprinkle cornstarch, instead of powder, on baby's bottom after washing and drying. This will help prevent diaper rash.

630 To prevent bathtub accidents, put a rubber bath mat over the edge of the tub. Use it for support when getting out of the tub, it will not slip! A wet face cloth over the edge of the tub also works very well as an anti-slip protection.

631 To avoid a bruise, rub the area immediately with pure essence of vanilla. There will be no black and blue marks.

632 To take the sting out of removing adhesive bandages, saturate the area with baby oil before pulling off bandages.

633 Clean a child's scrape with a red washcloth so the blood won't show.

634 Apply ice to a splinter before removing. It eliminates the fussing.

635 If you hit your thumb or finger accidentally with a hammer, immerse in cold water immediately. This will ease the pain and helps to prevent swelling.

FIRST AID

FIRST AID

636 To help prevent varicose veins, elevate your legs for 20 minutes each day.

637 If you need a hot water bottle in a hurry, fill a plastic two-litre soft drink bottle with hot water, screw on top and wrap in a towel.

GENERAL CLEANING

638 To make your own all-purpose cleaner combine ¼ cup baking soda, one cup household ammonia, ½ cup white vinegar and one gallon warm water. Mix in a large pail and use as needed. Store in clean Javex containers or other plastic jugs. Label with felt pen. Use at room temperature.

639 An excellent window cleaner or for washing walls, ceilings with gloss or semi-gloss paint, use a mixture of 1 cup plain ammonia, 3-4 quarts warm water, wash windows, wipe dry with paper towel. For walls and ceilings add about 2 cups sudsy ammonia.

640 Put your liquid cleaner (Mr. Clean etc.) in a spray bottle. It makes wipe-ups quick and easy and saves on the amount of liquid you use.

641 When doing general household cleaning, use a small toothbrush to clean small cracks.

642 If your sponge mop is starting to shred, wrap a sock over it.

643 Clamp old socks into a holder to make a great dry mop.

644 Cut the best parts of worn-out towels into squares and use as dishcloths and dusters.

645 Use old socks, underwear, T-shirts etc. for cleaning rags.

646 Make your own window and glass cleaner. Combine ½ cup household ammonia, two cups of 70 per cent isopropyl rubbing alcohol, one tsp. liquid dish detergent and add water to make one gallon. Store in an ice cream pail with lid and transfer to spray bottle as needed. (NOTE: Poison, keep away from children.)

647 One part vinegar and three parts water makes an excellent window cleaner.

648 For a perfect window washing solution, add ½ cup ammonia, ½ cup white vinegar and two tbsp. cornstarch to a bucket of warm water.

649 Money saving tip for window cleaner: combine, 3 tbsp. ammonia, 1 tbsp.vinegar, 1 cup water, 1 drop blue food coloring.

GENERAL CLEANING

GENERAL CLEANING

650 Make your own window and appliance cleaner by adding two tbsp. of vinegar, two to three drops of liquid dish detergent and blue food coloring to two quarts of water.

651 Never wash windows on a sunny day. They will dry too fast and streak.

652 When washing windows during cool weather, wet your cloth with automobile windshield washer solution. Wipe windows and dry with paper towels.

653 To clean mirrors and windows, mix two parts water to eight parts rubbing alcohol. There's no streaking, it evaporates quickly and it's inexpensive.

654 For sparkling windows and mirrors, use a mixture of one gallon of warm water and 1/4 cup of cornstarch. Wipe dry with a paper towel.

655 And for another window cleaner — dilute windshield washer fluid one-to-five with water, add one tbsp. vinegar and pour into spray bottle.

656 For cleaning large windows and patio doors get a bottle of rubbing alcohol and add a tsp. or two of straight ammonia. Mix and put in an empty sprayer bottle. This mixture cuts dirt and will not streak.

657 Use a little starch in the water to wash mirrors. It removes soil and gives a polish to the glass.

658 To make woodwork, windows and mirrors sparkle, clean with cold tea.

659 Place the crystals from your chandelier in a pillow case, fasten case securely and place in rack in dishwasher. They come out sparkling.

660 To dry clear decanters, use a hairblower or put over a heat register.

661 Clean flower vases with a solution of one tbsp. salt and one cup vinegar. Soak overnight.

68

662 Clean narrow-necked bottles by using a vinegar and water solution. Add some dry rice to produce a scouring effect when bottle is shaken.

663 Use toilet bowl cleaner to remove mineral deposits on glass bottles.

664 To remove hard water scale from the bottom of a drinking glass, fill above the scale line with pure vinegar and let sit until the glass is clean and clear.

665 Round typewriter erasers are excellent for removing paint spatters from window panes.

666 Scratches on glassware will disappear if polished with toothpaste.

667 Tiny chips can be taken out of fine crystal by rubbing the chipped edge with a fine silicon carbide paper (No. 320 grit).

668 A small nick in the rim of a glass can be smoothed with an emery board.

669 To remove price-tag glue, rub with a paper towel and a dab of peanut butter. The oil in the peanut butter cleans the glue off glass or plastic and leaves no stain.

670 Use vegetable oil to remove sticky tags from glass, ornaments or brass. It leaves no trace of glue.

GENERAL CLEANING

671 To remove fingerprints from photos, spray with hairspray and use soft cloth to buff.

672 For an inexpensive diamond cleaner, dip diamonds in full-strength vinegar, rinse with clear water and polish with a soft cloth.

673 To clean gold jewelry, use a solution of half ammonia and half water with a dash of liquid soap. Let jewelry soak in the solution for a few minutes and then take a soft toothbrush and clean around any etchings or stones. Rinse well and polish with a soft cloth. (DO NOT use on pearls or any soft stone.)

674 Dry-clean costume jewelry by placing in baking soda and brushing lightly.

675 When storing silver for an indefinite period, wrap a small piece of camphor with it to prevent tarnishing.

676 Stored silverware won't tarnish if you tuck a small piece of alum into your silver chest.

677 To clean small silver items, rub a small amount of toothpaste over them with a damp cloth and rinse clean.

678 To polish silver easily, gently rub with ashes from the fireplace.

679 Boil a few potato peels for several minutes in water. Let the mixture cool and then soak your silverware in it for 8 hours. Rub the silver gently while drying it.

680 To shine silver flatware, place in an enamel pan lined with aluminum foil, cover with boiling water, add three tbsp. baking soda and let stand for a few minutes. Rinse and dry. This method is not recommended for pieces with cemented-on handles or for silver with a carved or raised design, accented by a dark finish.

681 To clean brass, combine ¼ cup salt with enough vinegar to dissolve. Add flour to make a paste.

682 Polish brass with Worcestershire sauce and then brighten by rubbing with olive oil after each polishing.

683 To clean copper, use Worcestershire sauce. What surprising results you'll get!

684 A lemon peel dipped in salt will clean tarnished brass.

685 If brass isn't overly tarnished, wash it in water in which potatoes have been boiled.

686 To clean brass or copper, use a soft cloth and some ketchup. Clean off with a damp cloth and rub to polish.

687 To clean copper and brass, wash thoroughly then dip a soft cloth in vinegar and then in whiting or salt and scour the metal. Wash and dry, then rub with a soft cloth.

688 For an inexpensive copper cleaner mix together one tbsp. flour, one tbsp. salt and one tbsp. vinegar.

689 Mix together one-part salt to five-parts vinegar and pour into used detergent bottle. Use for cleaning copper.

690 Instead of using copper cleaner, you can clean copper-bottomed pots and other kitchen utensils with toothpaste and a damp cloth.

691 For all your cleaning chores – use VINEGAR! Use equal parts of vinegar and water in a spray bottle for doing mirrors, windows, pictur.es. Dampen a soft cloth with this solution for dusting. I use it on my grand piano! Great for getting scum out of bud vases or any glass container.

GENERAL CLEANING

692 Use used fabric softener sheets for dusting. They pick up all lint and dust and leave furniture clean.

693 To make your own dustcloths, put hot sudsy water into a large jar with two tsp. of turpentine. Shake jar and put some old rags inside. Let sit overnight, then wring out and hang to dry. These rags will clean off the dust and leave furniture shining.

694 A carwash glove serves as a perpetual furniture duster. Impregnated with polish, it will serve over and over before needing washing.

695 Keep an elastic band around your bottle of furniture polish to hold your cleaning cloth.

696 Keep an automobile brush with your household cleaning things. It's great for dusting underneath sofas, chairs, appliances and other hard-to-get-at corners.

697 For those popular, but high maintenance venetian blinds, rub a fabric softener sheet over the slats and it will repel the dust that so quickly seems to accumulate on them.

698 Clean your venetian blinds with a solution of one quart water, three tablespoons vinegar and two teaspoons liquid detergent. Wipe blinds with a damp cloth.

699 Heavily soiled blinds may be washed in the bathtub. Half fill the tub with lukewarm water, one cup liquid detergent and one-half cup vinegar. Swish blinds in tub, rinse with shower and hang from shower curtain rod.

700 Cheesecloth over the heat registers cuts down on dust.

701 To remove pet hair from furniture and pillows, dampen a sponge with a solution of warm water and glycerin or just use water. Squeeze the sponge thoroughly and lightly brush over furniture.

702 Homemade furniture polish: ½ cup vinegar, one cup boiled linseed oil, one cup turpentine, ¼ cup methylated spirits. Mix vinegar and oil gradually to a thick cream; then add turpentine and spirits. Bottle and shake well before using.

703 Put ordinary Vaseline on a soft cloth and apply and polish as you would furniture polish. The Vaseline soaks into the wood and restores dried-out furniture. It also brings out the grain and leaves a lasting natural lustre.

704 For old-fashioned furniture polish, combine one tablespoon vinegar, two tablespoons virgin olive oil, four cups water. Put in a spray bottle (recycled hair spray bottle, etc.) Spray on furniture and wipe dry. It gives a nice shine and removes build-up of commercial polishes.

705 Glycerin or olive oil on your dust rag removes dust easily and leaves items polished.

706 Baby oil makes ideal furniture polish, at less than half the cost of commercial polish.

707 For an inexpensive furniture polish, combine equal quantities of boiled flaxseed oil, white vinegar and turpentine. Shake together.

708 Water stains on a table can be removed with paste of cigarette ashes and butter or margarine. Rub with the grain of the wood.

709 To remove scratches in furniture, rub a peanut over the scratches.

710 Darken a small scratch in varnished wood with a walnut or pecan. The flaw almost disappears.

GENERAL CLEANING

711 Wet glasses, hot dishes, alcohol and perfume will leave white marks on wooden furniture. To remove the marks and restore the original color, use a solution of two parts alcohol, two parts turpentine and one part olive oil and rub it in well with a cloth.

712 To remove white heat marks on furniture, apply a thin paste of salad oil and salt. Let stand one to two hours, wipe off and polish.

713 To remove water marks from furniture, mix cigarette ashes with a little Vaseline and rub on spot.

714 Cover scratches on brown or cherry mahogany with old iodine which has turned brown. For red mahogany, use new iodine and for maple, try diluting iodine with denatured alcohol, half and half.

715 For burns on a wood table, swab the burn with nail polish remover, then gently scrape away with a dull knife until the burn is gone. Fill the indentation with layers of clear nail polish, then cover with regular furniture polish.

716 To remove stains from woodwork, put furniture oil on a cloth, then dab on a little baking soda and rub on the stain.

717 To clean wood panelling, remove any old furniture polish with Varsol or other petroleum solvent and a clean cloth. Buff with a dry cloth to remove streaks. From then on, just use a damp cloth or sponge and a drop or two of dish detergent to clean the panelling when necessary. Always buff with a dry cloth after cleaning.

718 To remove two-faced tape without damaging the wallboard, spray well with petroleum-based prewash spray and ease off with blunt-edged knife or spatula.

719 To whiten piano keys, wash with rubbing alcohol.

720 To prevent pottery from scratching the furniture, use some self-stick bunion pads on the bottoms of the pottery.

721 To prevent chairs scratching the floors, put self-stick bunion pads on the bottom of the chair legs.

722 Wax chair leg bottoms to prevent scratching the floor when chair is moved.

723 If an egg falls and breaks on the floor, sprinkle the egg generously with salt and let stand a short time. Then wipe up with a cloth or paper towel. It comes up clean and leaves no mess on the floor.

724 Before using a cloth to wax the floor, soak it in cold water and wring out. You will find that the cloth will not absorb the wax and you will save a good deal of wax which otherwise would have been wasted.

725 Instead of using commercial preparations, you can wax a floor by washing it with one gallon warm water to which two tbsp. furniture polish and ½ cup vinegar have been added. Unused portion can be bottled for future use.

726 Use liquid wax on rubber or vinyl mats.

727 When cleaning floors which have been waxed, put a small amount of vinegar in cold water. Wash floors with this. The cold water won't remove the wax and the vinegar will remove the dirt. It works and the floor retains its original shine.

728 Use ammonia to remove floor wax.

729 Before sweeping away broken glass, wet the end the broom. It will pick up small scattered pieces of glass which you can't see.

730 Put a coat of wax on your dustpan. Dust and dirt will slide off easily.

731 Remove tar from vinyl floor by rubbing it with butter or margarine. Wipe with a dry cloth.

732 Save old hairbrushes and use them to clean your vacuum, lint trap on your dryer or to dust behind radiators.

733 Reuse your vacuum bags by carefully slitting open the bottom with a razor blade or sharp scissors and emptying the bag. Then seal shut carefully with tape.

GENERAL CLEANING

734 Before you dust or vacuum, tape a small paper bag to your apron or belt so you can drop in stray pins, crayons, etc. which you find along the way.

735 To vacuum Christmas tree needles, put a pantihose leg on the nozzle. The vacuum will draw up the hose as well as the needles so you will have to hold the pantihose around the nozzle. When you are finished, just pull out pantihose and throw away. No need to worry about a plugged up vacuum hose.

736 Give carpets a liberal sprinkling of salt before vacuuming. It helps destroy moth larvae and brightens colors.

737 To get mud out of the carpet, sprinkle with cornstarch, let stand 15 minutes, then vacuum.

738 Most spots on carpet can be eliminated by rubbing a slice of white bread over the area, then vacuuming. The bread should be one or two days old.

739 For grease stains on carpet, sprinkle cornmeal on area, brush lightly, leave overnight and then vacuum.

740 To get a grease spot out of the kitchen carpet, sprinkle with baking soda, then shampoo and vacuum.

741 Use shaving cream as a spot remover for cleaning carpets. Wash it out with water or club soda.

742 To remove most stains from your carpet, sprinkle with salt and sponge out.

743 Use 7-Up or ginger ale to get grape, beet or strawberry stains out of the carpet.

744 To get red wine out of a carpet, throw towels on the wet stain, one at a time, letting the towels soak up as much of the wine as possible. Press gently on the towels to soak up wine from the bottom of the fibers. Then put clean towels over the spot and stack books on them overnight. In the morning all the wine will be completely absorbed. The secret is do not rub, just apply gentle pressure.

745 To remove fresh spills and pet stains from carpet, blot spill with paper towel, saturate with soda water, let sit for five minutes and blot with paper towel. The stain will be gone.

746 Instead of using expensive brand-name carpet deodorizing products, sprinkle baking soda on the carpet, wait 10-15 minutes, then vacuum. The baking soda absorbs pet and smoke odors and leaves a fresh smell.

747 Add a cotton ball saturated with your favorite scent to your vacuum cleaner bag. As you vacuum, a fresh aroma will fill the air.

748 To get rid of pet odors on carpets, use a spray bottle containing white vinegar and spray the area.

749 To prevent static shock from carpeting, mix one-part liquid fabric softener with five-parts water in a spray bottle. Mist the carpet lightly.

750 When you want to move furniture in a carpeted room, but hesitate because of indents caused by the furniture, place a damp cloth on the indentation and place an iron (on low setting) on top of the cloth. Hold just long enough to heat. This will relift the carpet fibres and then simply brush the fibres to their original position.

751 Here's an easy way to wash walls. To one gallon of warm water, add two tbsp. baking soda, four oz. vinegar and four oz. ammonia. Use a sponge and wash from the bottom of the wall up to the ceiling to prevent streaks. You do not have to rinse.

752 A cloth dampened with turpentine will remove crayon marks from painted walls or wallpaper.

GENERAL CLEANING

753 Crayon marks can be removed from painted walls by rubbing them with a cloth dampened with lighter fluid.

754 Crayon can be removed from walls by coating the mark with toothpaste and letting it set for approximately 15 minutes before wiping clean with a dry cloth.

755 Toothpaste will take ballpoint ink or crayon off walls. Just rub on then wipe off with a damp cloth.

756 Black marks on walls can be removed with a soft, damp cloth and some toothpaste.

757 To remove grease spots on wallpaper, make a paste of cornstarch and water, let it remain on the spot until dry, then brush off.

758 To clean nonwashable wallpaper, rub gently with an art gum eraser or a crustless piece of bread.

759 Windowsills are easy to clean if you give them a coat of wax. Wax protects the paint and dirt wipes off in a jiffy.

760 You can scent the house by simmering cloves and cinnamon on the stove. It also adds humidity. The same spices can be used over and over again for this purpose.

761 Put a teaspoon of vanilla in a small pot of water and boil to take odors out of the kitchen.

762 Dab a cottonball in wintergreen oil and hide somewhere in the room. The room will stay fresh for months.

763 A small container of vinegar left in any room of the house keeps the room smelling fresh even when the house is closed up for a while.

764 Add vinegar occasionally to the water in your humidifier. It will keep the air fresher.

765 An inexpensive and quick method of freshening up your home is to apply vanilla extract to a cloth and wipe on lights in various rooms throughout the house. A fresh, clean aroma is released when you turn on the lights.

766 To remove smoke from a room, dip a towel in equal parts vinegar and water. Wring out and whirl gently over your head.

767 To stop butts burning in the ashtray, line the bottom with one inch of baking soda.

768 To rid tap water of chlorine smell, fill a pitcher and let water stand overnight.

769 To ensure a pleasant, clean smell from your garburator, grind lemon rinds or add a few drops of lemon juice after you turn off the garburator.

770 New paint odor can be disposed of by placing a large plate filled with salt in the room.

771 Drains and toilet bowls can be deodorized and sanitized with vinegar.

772 Put a few drops of vanilla in a small glass and place in the refrigerator to banish food odors.

773 Baking powder placed in the refrigerator and freezer takes away odors and keeps the refrigerator fresh.

774 A teaspoon of lemon extract in your cleaning water will eliminate bad smells in your refrigerator.

GENERAL CLEANING

GENERAL CLEANING

775 To deodorize refrigerator, cut a raw potato in half and place inside the refrigerator, cut side up. Just pare off when it turns black.

776 The least expensive refrigerator deodorizer is two charcoal briquettes.

777 Place a piece of barbecue charcoal inside the freezer to eliminate stale freezer odors.

778 If a plastic storage container has an unpleasant smell, fill it with water, add a few drops of vanilla extract and let stand overnight.

779 To remove damp and musty odors in closets, place used coffee grounds in an open container in the closet. This can also be used to the refrigerator to control odors.

780 Clean mildewed surfaces with a rag soaked in fresh lemon juice and salt.

781 Remove mildew from a leather suitcase by wiping it down with a cloth moistened in a solution of equal parts rubbing alcohol and water. Dry in an airy room.

782 Clean sliding door gliders, then run either parafin wax or a candle over them to facilitate easier, quieter opening and closing.

783 Clean your telephone with rubbing alcohol to keep it looking new.

784 To clean a soft rubber eraser which has become soiled from use, rub it against an ink eraser. This cleaning action works both ways as the soft eraser will remove smudges from the harder, more abrasive ink eraser.

KITCHEN CLEANING

785 When liquid dish detergent container appears empty, add small amount of water to it and you'll have enough for a few more washes.

786 Add a bit of vinegar to your dishwater. This will cut the grease, allowing you to use a cheaper brand of detergent.

787 Put one tbsp. of bleach in your water when washing dishes. It kills germs.

788 One tbsp. of bleach in the dishwater will keep the dishcloth clean and smelling fresh.

789 Use hot water for washing dishes, but make certain you wear rubber gloves.

790 Use baking soda to clean Corning-type dishes.

791 Brighten discolored enamel ware with a paste of salt and vinegar.

792 If you have burned food on the bottom of a cooking pan, let sit overnight with vinegar and Comet covering the burned area. It wipes out easily the next day.

793 To give burned food the brush off, let a mixture of half water and half vinegar soak in the pan overnight. The burned food comes off easily the next day with a light scouring.

794 To clean a scorched pan, put soap and cold water into the pan and simmer. You can remove scorched spots without scratching the surface of the pan.

795 When you scorch a pan, try sprinkling dry baking soda over the scorch. Let stand awhile and clean as usual.

796 To remove burned-on food stuck to enamel saucepans, place a strong salt solution in the pot and let soak several hours. Cover the pot, place it on the stove and bring solution to a slow boil. This usually removes the burned food safely.

797 A few drops of bleach in lukewarm water will remove tea stains from cups and teapot.

798 A paste of baking soda and water will remove coffee and tea stains from porcelain and china.

799 To clean a coffee pot, use one denture tablet in cold water and soak overnight.

800 To remove coffee film from thermos bottle, pour in one tbsp. raw rice and one cup of warm water. Shake well and rinse.

801 To remove brown grease marks from pots, chrome burner rings, etc., soak in ammonia overnight.

802 To remove rust from baking pans, dip a raw potato in any cleaning powder, then scour the pans.

803 Rust can be removed from a knife blade by plunging it into an onion and leaving it there for an hour or so. Work blade back and forth a few times and wash in soap and water.

804 To remove food stuck to a casserole dish, fill with boiling water and add two tbsp. baking soda or salt.

805 When purchasing meat wrapped in plastic mesh, save the mesh. Wrap the mesh in a ball, secure with a plastic garbage bag tie and use as a pot scrubber.

806 To preserve plastic pot scrubbers, place them in plastic mesh grape bags. Twist and slip the mesh bag back to double it and tie a knot in the end. The pot scrubbers will last twice as long.

KITCHEN CLEANING

KITCHEN CLEANING

807 A small ball of tinfoil works well to clean your pans inside and out.

808 Keep a toothbrush in your kitchen. It's great for cleaning small areas such as beaters and graters.

809 Steel wool soap pads won't rust if you keep them in the freezer or refrigerator.

810 To keep an SOS pad from rusting, put one or two teaspoons of baking soda in the dish in which the pad is kept. The pad will remain rust-free until it is worn out.

811 Cut an SOS pad into four pieces. It lasts much longer because using the whole pad causes it to rust before the next use.

812 Fill soap cups in dishwasher only half-full. This saves on dishwashing soap and your glasses will not get water marked and scarred.

813 Use equal amounts of dishwasher soap and baking soda in your dishwasher. Your dishes and silver will be cleaner and so will the machine.

814 To remove scum from glassware, add ½ cup bleach to wash cycle in dishwasher and ½ cup vinegar to the rinse. The vinegar neutralizes the bleach.

815 If your dishwasher needs cleaning, use powdered laundry bleach instead of dishwasher detergent in an empty machine. This will clean and disinfect the dishwasher.

816 To remove lime buildups in your dishwasher, put ¾ cup laundry bleach into empty dishwasher and run it through first wash. After this drains, add two cups vinegar and run through the rinse cycle, but not the drying cycle. Reset the dishwasher for a full cycle, using dish detergent.

817 If the inside of your dishwasher is discolored due to iron deposits, run washer through a cycle using ¼ cup of Oxalic Acid Crystals (can be purchased at the drugstore). Then run through a second cycle with just water.

818 If your dishwasher or dishes become stained from hard water, just run a package of Tang orange juice crystals through the dishwasher with the stained dishes in it.

819 When water discharges from a portable dishwasher into the sink, a fine spray splashes over the sink and sometimes onto the floor. To prevent this, cut out the bottom of a quart-size milk carton and slip this on the discharge pipe of the dishwasher. The water will flow directly through the carton into the drain.

820 When using the automatic dishwasher, open the door and turn the cycle to off when the washing cycle has finished and let the dishes air dry.

821 For a sparkling white kitchen sink, place paper towels across the bottom of your sink and saturate with household bleach. Let sit for at least a half hour.

822 For fragrant, clean sinks, pour ½ cup baking soda, followed by one cup vinegar, down the drain. Let bubble 15 minutes, then rinse with warm water.

823 Instead of expensive cleaners, use baking soda to clean your stainless steel sink.

824 Club soda can be used to shine a stainless steel sink.

KITCHEN CLEANING

825 To remove alkali corrosion around taps, etc., use straight vinegar.

826 Kitchen taps can be kept free of water spots if you polish them with a coat of liquid wax.

827 Stainless steel sinks may be brightened by using a cloth dampened with vinegar.

828 To get rid of rust marks on stainless steel sinks, rub with lighter fluid.

829 Clean rusty sink stains by using cream of tartar and a few drops of hydrogen peroxide.

830 A cloth dampened with vinegar will remove rust stains caused by leaky faucets.

831 Place a marble in your tea kettle to prevent the kettle from scaling.

832 White vinegar works well as a scale remover for electric kettles and steam irons.

833 To clean inside of teapot, if scales gather in the pot or spout, pour 1½ to two tbsp. of Spic and Span into empty pot. Fill to brim with boiling water, let stand until cool and rinse well.

834 To clean thermos bottles, fill with water, add 1 tsp. baking soda. Let stand overnight.

835 Run a piece of paper towel through the cutting mechanism of your electric can opener. It will absorb the grease and grime.

836 A damp cloth dipped in cigarette ash will clean the bottom of your electric frying pan.

837 Nail polish remover will take off any plastic which has melted onto the toaster.

838 Dry baking soda and a damp cloth will remove stains from chrome appliances.

839 Use baking soda to clean chrome and the glass door of oven.

840 Before starting to clean your oven, use Lustre Sheen cream hand cleaner with lanolin underneath your fingernails. Also coat your hands lightly. Your hands will come clean easily after the job is done.

841 Sprinkle soda generously on the bottom of your oven, let sit for one hour and wipe clean.

842 If your oven isn't too dirty, a saucer full of household ammonia placed in the oven the night before cleaning will soften the residue. (BEWARE of the vapors when cleaning.)

843 To clean oven racks, put in bathtub with ½ cup dishwasher detergent. Soak for 30-45 minutes. No scrubbing required.

844 To easily clean a broiler pan, sprinkle the hot pan heavily with dry laundry detergent. Cover with a dampened paper towel and let sit for a while.

845 To clean oven and barbecue grills, put in bathtub with ammonia and water.

846 Put an open container of ammonia in a plastic garbage bag with your barbecue grill. Set in the sun for a couple of hours. Take out grill and rinse clean.

847 To clean barbecue and oven grills, place in bathtub with dishwasher soap and hot water.

KITCHEN CLEANING

848 To clean your whole stove from top to bottom, put all removable parts from your stove and oven into a large garbage bag and pour in a couple cups of ammonia. Seal the bag with a twist tie and let it sit for several hours or overnight. Rinse clean with warm water.

849 Put tinfoil, shiny side down, on your gas grill. Turn on high for 10 minutes. When cool, remove foil and the grill will be clean.

850 If something catches fire in your oven, sprinkle the fire generously with salt or baking soda. This will stop the flame and smoke immediately.

851 Place wax paper under ice cube trays in the freezer so they won't stick.

852 To clean counter tops, scrub with a paste of baking soda and water. Let sit for 1/2 hour and wipe with a wet sponge.

853 Ammonia and water cleans grease from cupboards. Use one-part ammonia to five-parts water.

854 To prevent rust stains under your metal canisters when water is spilled on the counter, keep your canisters sitting on plastic container lids. The lids will raise the canisters about 1/2 inch off the counter.

855 Keep the top of kitchen cabinets clean. Unroll clear plastic wrap and cover the cupboard top. When cleaning time comes, simply roll up plastic wrap and throw in the garbage. Replace with fresh wrap.

856 To clean a stained bread board, sprinkle with salt and rub it all over with the cut side of a lemon.

857 To remove onion smell from breadboard, sprinkle board with baking soda and scrub.

858 Once every six months cover your chopping board with vegetable oil and let stand overnight. Then, wipe off the oil. The board will last indefinitely.

859 To keep wooden salad bowls from drying and cracking, wipe them inside and out with a paper towel soaked with cooking oil. Do this in the evening and in the morning wipe off excess oil. Repeat about once a month.

BATHROOM CLEANING

860 Wipe a little glycerin (available in drug stores) on windows and bathroom mirrors and buff with a soft cloth to keep them from steaming up.

861 For a fast shine to your glass shower doors, wipe them with a sponge containing white vinegar. It cuts soap film quickly.

862 Use baking soda mixed with liquid dish detergent and water to scour the tub and walls and doors of the shower.

863 Hang a small squeegee in the shower stall. After each shower, clean the sides and door of the stall. It will always look clean and big cleaning jobs will be eliminated.

864 Clean bathroom tiles with vinegar which has been poured into a spray bottle.

865 One of the easiest ways to clean bathroom walls is to run hot water in the bathtub and shut the door for five minutes. Steam will form on the walls and ceilings and loosen the dirt, which can then be wiped with a dry, clean cloth.

866 Shiny tiles can be achieved easily if you polish them with car wax after washing and drying thoroughly.

867 To remove yellow stains which often appear on white bathtubs, wipe lightly with a mixture of salt and turpentine.

868 The same enzyme presoak that takes stains out of fabric will clean unsightly spots from porcelain sinks. Soak sink and garments at the same time.

869 The rough, grainy texture which forms in bathtubs can be removed by soaking with vinegar.

870 To remove stains from old bathtubs, use a "fine" automotive polishing compound.

871 Use undiluted ammonia to remove bath oil rings from the bathtub.

872 Get rid of mildew around tiles and fixtures by washing with a solution of 1½ cups of bleach diluted in 4 quarts of warm water.

873 To get rid of mildew stains on sinks, tubs and tiles, pour on bleach, let sit for a few minutes, then rinse.

874 To eliminate mineral deposits which often block shower heads, unscrew the end of the shower head and boil it in white vinegar for approximately 15-20 minutes. Let it cool thoroughly. Rinse well in cold water and re-install it.

875 Shine chrome in the bathroom with a cloth dampened with vinegar. Let dry, then polish with a soft cloth.

876 Use hydrogen peroxide in shower door tracks to loosen the hardened scum. When it bubbles up, run a cotton swab along the track and flush with a glass of water.

877 To get the grime and mildew out of shower curtains, fill your washing machine with warm water, add detergent and ½ cup bleach. Let the machine run a few seconds, then put the shower curtains in, along with three or four towels. Let the cycle finish.

878 To get soap film and grime off vinyl shower curtains, spray them down with a vinegar/water solution and then wash them in the washing machine with another cup of vinegar and regular detergent.

879 Use wintergreen oil as a bathroom deodorant. Soak a cotton ball with the oil and place in a glass container. It will last for months.

880 Coat your metal bathroom scales with pastewax to ward off rust from water splashes.

881 Place a denture-cleaning tablet in the toilet bowl and let it dissolve. This is an easy, inexpensive way to help keep the bowl clean.

882 Muratic acid works well for cleaning extra stubborn stains in toilet bowls. (REMEMBER: Caution must be used when using acid.)

883 Put a scoop of Tang in the toilet bowl and let sit for a couple of hours. It eliminates toilet bowl stains, leaving the toilet clean and fresh smelling.

884 Pour leftover cola drinks into your toilet bowl. Let soak, then flush and the bowl will sparkle.

BATHROOM CLEANING

885 Save old toothbrushes for cleaning around difficult areas in the bathroom.

886 A sponge makes a great soap dish.

887 To keep soap from melting in a wet soap dish, put a pop bottle cover on the soap to keep it from touching the surface of the dish.

PANTIHOSE

888   Store onions in old pantihose or nylons.

889   Use old knee-high hose to dry and store garlic in a cool dry place.

890   Cut the elastic tops off old pantihose and use them for closing boxes, big packages, etc. They work very well on many different things.

891   Cut a thin strip around a pair of discarded pantihose, stretch and use to sew buttons on coats or children's clothing.

892   To save a lot of work for no extra cost, take a white nylon stocking leg, cut off the foot, boil the hose a few minutes, then dry. Tie one end of the leg and use this bag to hold the bread stuffing for chicken or turkey. When poultry is cooked, the dressing can easily be removed.

893   Wash old pantihose and use as stuffing for stuffed toys (either as replacement stuffing or for use in homemade toys).

894   Spray Static Cling to your pantihose before putting them on. They're easier to pull on and underclothes will not cling.

895   Put a folded fabric softener sheet in a small plastic bag and place in your purse. If static cling strikes while you're out, rub the sheet over slip, pantihose or other items of clothing. A single sheet can be used many times.

896   Wear gloves when putting on pantihose and save your pantihose from snags and holes caused by rough or long fingernails.

897   Pantihose will last longer if you freeze them before wearing. Wet, wring dry, place in a plastic bag and put in the freezer. After the pantihose have frozen solid, thaw and hang to dry.

898   Always buy two of your favorite pantihose — same shade and texture. When one leg runs, simply cut it off and save the rest until a leg runs on the second pair. Then, by wearing both pairs, with one leg each, you've created a new pair at no extra cost.

899   Using hairspray on the heels and toes of sandalfoot pantihose will help them last longer.

PANTIHOSE

PANTIHOSE

900   Pantihose and nylons make an excellent filling for quilts or cushions. The quilts and cushions are easy to wash and dry quickly.

901   Use pantihose to strain paint.

902   Add one tsp. of vinegar to the rinse water for pantihose to help them retain their elasticity.

903   Use old pantihose to tie plants to stakes.

904   Save the white cardboards from pantihose and use them for writing grocery lists and notes.

905   If your fan belt snaps, use a pair of pantihose as a substitute. Cut to fit.

906   When you have pantihose with only one good leg, cut off the good leg and save it until you get another of the same color and use them with a garter belt.

907   If you forget to wash out your pantihose ahead of time and need them right away, wash them and place in your hair-dryer hood. Turn on dryer and your hose will be dry in minutes.

908   When hanging pantihose outside on the line to dry, put a teaspoon in each foot. They won't blow over the line and get snagged.

ENERGY

909 Make certain that everyone turns off the lights when leaving the room. For extra incentive, charge 25 cents when a person leaves a room without shutting off the lights.

910 If your children have the bad habit of leaving the basement lights on, unscrew half the light bulbs in the basement. Now, if they leave them on it's not so wasteful or costly. The light bulbs left should provide plenty of light for playing.

911 A dimmer switch will save on light bills.

912 To save money, reduce the wattage of the bulbs you use.

913 It is more economical to use one large bulb rather than several small ones. A 100-watt bulb gives as much light as six 25-watt bulbs, but uses less than ⅔ the power.

914 When your night light bulb needs replacing, use a Christmas tree lightbulb — it's the same size.

915 Don't forget the lightbulbs when dusting. A dusty bulb will give off up to 50 per cent less light.

916 Use electric tea kettles, electric skillets and electric woks. They use less energy than stove top kettles, skillets and woks.

917 To save energy, do not preheat the oven before cooking casseroles or meat dishes.

918 For foods which require a long cooking time, it is more economical to use the oven than a burner on top of the stove.

919 Conserve energy by cooking the entire meal in the oven.

920 When cooking dinner in the oven, cook your canned vegetables by removing the label, taking off the lid and cooking in the tin can in the oven for about 15 minutes.

921 When baking, oven heat can be lowered 25 degrees if you use glass or ceramic baking dishes, which retain heat better than other materials.

922 Do not fill the kettle to the brim before boiling if only a few cups of water are needed. Boil only what you need.

ENERGY

923 Operating the dishwasher only once a day will consume less water and electricity.

924 To save on power, wash bath towels in cold water.

925 Partially dry bath towels in the dryer, then hang on chair backs or a clotheshorse to finish the job. This will save energy and will add humidity to the house.

926 Throw a dry bath towel into the dryer when drying a load. Laundry will dry a lot quicker, therefore saving power and wear on the dryer.

927 Instead of using the dryer, hang clothes outside to dry. In the winter, set up a clothes line in your basement.

928 Clean the dryer vent after every load to reduce energy use.

929 By purchasing a simple dryer vent control device, you can use the heat from the dryer for your basement or garage.

930 Use a 24-hour timer for your car block heater and interior warmer.

931 Installing a transient voltage surge suppressor at the electrical panel, could save money when using household appliances.

932 Use your bathroom fans sparingly in the winter. The fans remove warm air.

933 Run the furnace fan constantly during cold weather to reduce your heating bill.

934 Keep your furnace well tuned. A slipping belt can reduce the efficiency of your furnace by as much as 50 per cent.

935 Be certain your furnace has the proper amount of oxygen for maximum heat from your fuel.

936 Place aluminum foil behind each of your radiators. It will reflect heat back into the room instead of allowing the wall to absorb it.

937 Turn down the thermostat when you go out for the day.

938 Spray the furnace filter with furniture polish to increase the amount of dust it picks up.

939 Before retiring for the night, turn down your thermostat to 16-17° C (60-65° F).

940 To save fuel costs, install a set-back thermostat so that the temperature is maintained at a lower level while sleeping or when no one is home during the day. The initial investment is paid back in a short time through lower heating bills.

941 Close off heat and doors to unused rooms.

942 Keep your closet doors closed. There is no need to heat or cool them.

943 Cover your basement windows with some inexpensive material for the winter so heat is not lost through the glass and frame.

944 Draw your drapes closed and open only during sunny periods to conserve heat in the winter.

945 In the winter, block off radiators and open drapes on the sunny side of the house. This will keep the rooms on that side of the house warm.

946 On older homes, use plastic inside or outside to cover windows and frames to help cut drafts and cold.

ENERGY

ENERGY

947 Seal your windows in the winter to conserve heat.

948 If you have a milk chute which is not in use, pack it with fibreglass insulation to prevent drafts and frost buildup.

949 White foam meat trays can be washed, cut to size and fitted under wall switches etc. to prevent drafts.

950 Remove baseboards and caulk crack between wall and floor to prevent drafts along outside walls.

951 Make certain that your house is properly insulated and all air drafts plugged to prevent heat loss in the winter.

952 To help stop heat loss from the foundation of your house during the winter, shovel three or four feet of snow up against the side of the house to act as insulation.

953 Insulating the outside walls of your basement will pay for itself after three winters.

954 Keep blinds pulled down and drapes closed in the summer to keep the house cool and cut down on air conditioner use.

955 Keep your hot water heater in the mid range.

956 Turning down your hot water heater several degrees can save you a great deal of money over a year and it could also save you from scalds.

957 If you have to run the water forever until it gets hot, wrap your hot water pipes in an easy-to-apply foam blanket, available at hardware or building supply stores. Not only will you save on the water bill, but your hot water heating costs will be reduced too.

958 Adjust the float on your toilet so that you use less water when flushing.

959 Set a liner inside your toilet tank to conserve water.

960 Take a five minute shower (50 liters) instead of a bath (150 liters). Remember that less than 1% of Earth's water is available for our use.

961 Turn your water valves on and off every six months to keep them in working order. A stuck valve can cause a flood.

962 Have a timer near the telephone in order to limit long-distance phone bills. Set the timer for a predetermined length and stick to it.

ENERGY

PLANTS

963 Cut flowers from the garden in late evening or early morning. Use sharp shears and take water to the garden and plunge flowers in at once. Cut stems under water on the diagonal so they will not take in air but will absorb moisture well.

964 A solution of two tbsp. vinegar and three tsp. sugar to a quart of water will help cut flowers last longer.

965 Cut flowers will last longer if you keep them in equal parts of water and 7-Up with ½ tsp. of chlorine bleach added to each quart of this solution.

966 To keep fresh cut flowers lasting longer, add a few drops of chlorine bleach to the water, which will also stay fresh and odorless.

967 Drop a copper penny in the water with tulips so they will stand erect and not open wide.

968 When putting tulips in a vase, add vodka to the water to make them stand up straight and last longer.

969 To keep cut roses and woody-stemmed flowers lasting almost twice as long, cut the stems diagonally and pound the ends of the stems with a mallet.

970 Put a piece of charcoal in the water and cut flowers won't develop a bad odor when the stems begin to rot.

971 Homemade plant food: To one gallon of water (preferably rainwater or melted snow) add one tbsp. household ammonia, one tbsp. baking powder, one tbsp. saltpeter, one tbsp. druggist sulfur, two tbsp. Epsom salts, one rusty nail (or one Femiron tablet) and two tbsp. liquid soap. Use once a month to perk up your plants. For acid-loving plants add five tbsp. black coffee or four drops of white vinegar to the above recipe.

972 For plants which require acid soil, you may add a few drops of lemon juice or leftover tea water once a week.

973 To ensure that your house plants get enough nitrogen, water once a month with a solution of one seven-gram envelope of gelatin dissolved in one quart of water.

974 Sulphate of ammonia — one ounce to two gallons of water — prepared the evening before watering, is an excellent fertilizer for verbenas and other plants.

975 Geraniums bloom more often if you sprinkle 1 tablespoon of Epsom salts on the soil around them.

976 Save the water from boiling eggs. It is filled with minerals and excellent for your plants.

977 Throw your broken egg shells into a large container and fill with water. Let sit for a week, then discard the egg shells and use the water to feed your plants.

978 A birth control pill dissolved in one quart of water will help ferns grow faster and stronger.

979 Besides regular water, once a month dissolve an Aspirin in a cup of tea and feed to plants.

980 Spider plant, golden pothos or syngonium act as houseplant air cleaners.

981 Weak tea or water with a couple of drops of ammonia and dish soap makes an excellent plant spray. It cleans the plant and keeps pests away.

982 To get rid of indoor plant bugs, put a few drops of liquid detergent in the water when you water your plants. When the bugs go into the soil at night, they should die.

983 A small square of Vapona Strip, placed on the soil of a plant, will quickly get rid of spider mites.

984 Flytraps: If you have tiny flies around the house from potatoes, plants, etc., take a yellow plastic margarine or cottage cheese container and cut strips out of it. Coat strips with Vaseline and place in plant pots. The little flies come flying to the strips, get stuck to the Vaseline and trapped there. These flies are attracted to the color yellow.

985 To brighten leaves on a plant, dip a cottonball in milk and wash each leaf. They will shine better than with costly commercial products.

986 To keep the leaves on your indoor plants looking green and healthy, rub them with castor oil or mineral oil.

PLANTS

PLANTS

987 Put one tbsp. glycerin in the water for your houseplants. It will make the leaves shine.

988 Wipe plants with a mixture of a little mayonnaise and a little water. You'll have lots of shine and less dust.

989 Never put clay pots directly on wooden furniture because water will seep through the porous clay.

990 Use cottage cheese and yogurt lids for inexpensive plant pot stands.

991 To water your plants (if they are in clay pots which have drainage holes) while you are on holidays, set the plants on bricks in the bathtub and fill tub brick-high with water.

992 If you are going away for about a week, fill the bathtub with about ¼-inch of water. Set each of your plants on a saucer so that the pot doesn't touch the water. Cover the whole tub with a drycleaning bag.

993 If you can't get someone to water your plants while you are away, put all your household plants beside a large bowl of water. Drop ends of yarn into the container of water and then lay the other ends across the stalks of the plants. Capillary action of the water will carry enough moisture to keep the plants fresh.

994 White azalea will last longer than other colors.

995 To have fresh parsley and other spices all winter, plant and grow in flowerpots in the house.

996 Take an old, pithy cooking onion which is sprouting and plant it in a pot. Set in the window or outside and it will continue to grow tops. Just snip off for salads or soups.

997 For inexpensive houseplants, grow your own from avocado pits, orange pits, carrot and pineapple tops.

998 Always use moist soil only for transplanting or repotting to avoid root damage. Moisten soil the day before and dampen peat moss several days before use.

999 Egg shells make a good substitute for pebbles in houseplants. They promote drainage and also add lime to the soil.

1000 Styrofoam packing chips are good substitutes for the pebbles usually used as the drainage layer in the bottom of plant and flower pots. They permit an easy flow of water, are indestructible and add almost nothing to the weight of the container.

1001 When repotting plants, place a coffee filter in the pot before filling it with soil. The filter stops the soil from leaking out of the bottom of the pot and making a mess in the saucer.

1002 Use chipped or broken cups, bowls, vases or old ornaments for small houseplants.

1003 Save empty egg cartons to start your spring seedlings in.

1004 You can use old ice cube trays as plant starters. Leaving the sectional part in the tray, press a mixture of soil in each section and plant one or two seeds (depending on kind) in each. Water well. When ready to transplant, gently lift sec tional part and each plant will come out easily.

1005 Plant seedlings in styrofoam cups. They are economical and the plants are easy to remove when it's time for transplanting.

PLANTS

PLANTS

1006   Save empty two-quart milk cartons (cut in half) to use as seed flats when starting garden transplants.

1007   Store flower bulbs over the winter in discarded nylon stockings. Hang the bulb-filled stockings in a dry place so the air can circulate through them and prevent the bulbs from molding.

1008   Whitewash the inside of your window boxes before filling with earth. This will prevent the boxes from rotting and will help keep away insects.

1009   Window boxes won't splatter windows if you put a shallow layer of gravel over the dirt.

1010   When transplanting tomato and cucumber plants, put a handful of ashes around each plant. This will stop cutworms, acts as a fertilizer and keeps the soil loose.

1011   When planting tomatoes and cucumbers use about 1 tsp. of blood meal or bone meal. Add about 1 tsp. per plant every 2 weeks during growing season, until freeze-up. Yields will be great.

1012   To grow the biggest juiciest, most abundant tomatoes, sprinkle 1 teaspoon of Epsom salts into each planting hole. (It's the magnesium in the Epsom salts that works the magic!)

1013 Scatter onions throughout the garden instead of planting them in rows so root maggots can't simply travel from plant to plant.

1014 Before planting onion sets, let them stand 24 hours in a solution of one cup Javex to one quart water. No more maggots.

1015 Save garden space by planting radishes in the carrot and lettuce rows. They help mark the slow-germinating carrot row and they help protect lettuce from bugs.

1016 If you want to get more out of your vegetable garden, try interplanting. To interplant, you put rows of fast-growing vegetables between rows of slow-growing ones. All the crops are planted at once, but they'll mature at different times. Simply set rows of fast-growing crops such as lettuce, spinach or radishes between slower crops like tomatoes or cucumbers. The speedy ones will be ready for harvest just about the time when the slow ones get large and need the room.

1017 When you are cleaning out your garden, wash your carrots in your automatic washer, cold water and gentle cycle. Remove carrots, dry and store in plastic bags in the refrigerator or cool place. Works great!

1018 When planting mint, after plants have grown a few inches, cut tops and bottoms from large (48 oz.) juice cans and sink cans into the ground around mint plants. This prevents mint roots from spreading all over the garden or plant area.

1019 Banana skins, placed just below the surface of the soil, rot quickly and supply calcium, magnesium, sulphur, phosphorous, sodium and silica — marvellous for roses and flowers.

1020 Save all your egg shells in a plastic bag. Crush with a rolling pin and sprinkle around your rose bushes and flowers. They'll keep the bugs away.

1021 Save all your vegetable peels and scraps to make humus or just throw them on the garden in the winter.

PLANTS

PLANTS

1022 A Compost Pile for small gardens: Use a wooden box, kept outside. Add peat moss if you have no soil. Add water. Add potato peels, lettuce, egg shells, apple peels, etc. Mix with peat moss. This makes a good additive soil for house plants, etc.

1023 Cutworm moths seek out mulch and crop residues as egg-laying sites in early spring. Clean up the garden thoroughly every fall and till the soil in early spring to effectively eliminate the larvae.

1024 If you have a cutworm problem in your lawn, add three ounces of dish detergent to a two-gallon watering can filled with water. Cover your lawn well, then water in the evening. This will force the cutworms to the surface during the night and they will dry out in the morning sun.

1025 Pests or cutworms in the garden? Plant marigold seeds in a border around the garden. This makes a pleasant area and keeps most harmful insects away from your vegetables.

1026 To keep your garden free of cutworms, save wood ashes from your fireplace or campfire and work them into the soil. This doesn't harm the earthworms.

1027 To keep out slugs, put a band of sawdust around your garden.

1028 To make an ant destroyer, mix together 1/2 cup water and 1 cup sugar. Boil for 5 minutes. Add 1 tbsp. Borax. Put the liquid in bottle caps or small flat containers and place in the garden, under trees or in areas protected from the rain.

1029 Garlic powder on the inside of your garden cabbage will keep away cabbage butterflies.

1030 Plant dill near your tomatoes. It lures caterpillars away from prize crops.

1031 Make your own safe insecticide by adding 2 tablespoons of soap flakes to a quart of water and douse the infested leaves. Use ordinary soap flakes (not laundry detergent) or Safer's insecticidal soap and apply the solution with a watering can.

1032 Rid outdoor plants of pests by mixing a liberal dose of soap flakes, ¼ tsp. vinegar and approximately four cups water in the plant mister and spraying on affected areas.

1033 Prevent worms in your garden onions. Save coffee grounds and let dry. Place at the bottom of each row when planting onions.

1034 Tinfoil spread on the ground around plants will keep cats away.

1035 Use broken cassette tapes to tie plants to stakes.

1036 Water your lawn in the evening to get less evaporation.

1037 To kill grass and unwanted weeds growing between cement sections, pour salted, boiling water over them.

1038 Vinegar will destroy grass in sidewalk and driveway cracks.

PLANTS

MISCELLANEOUS

1039 Save your old dishcloths and linen tea towels. They make excellent floor rags.

1040 Save on paper towels by using old terry tea towels to dry vegetables or for quick mop-ups in the kitchen. Wash and reuse indefinitely.

1041 Wax your ashtrays. Ashes will not cling and they can be easily cleaned with facial tissue or paper towel.

1042 Nail polish remover will remove gummed labels from ornaments, dishes etc.

1043 Hairspray will help remove sticky residue left by price tags.

1044 To remove a special label for a coupon offer, wet a paper towel and wrap around the jar, then place the jar inside a plastic bag and twist-tie shut. Let stand overnight and the label will come loose easily.

1045 An overload of suds in the sink settles with a sprinkle of salt.

1046 Wash used Ziploc/Baggie food bags and reuse time and time again.

1047 Save empty plastic bread bags for storing other foods.

1048 To save the numerous plastic bags which come into your home, take an empty cardboard roller from foil or waxpaper and roll the plastic bags onto the roller. They will store neatly in a drawer.

1049 Save plastic wrap from meat or bakery goods and roll on an empty paper towel roll. Reuse the wrap as needed.

1050 To keep from wasting plastic wrap, because it sticks to the roll and peels off unevenly, put it in the freezer a few minutes before using.

1051 Store your plastic wrap in the refrigerator to keep it from sticking to itself.

1052 Thoroughly wash plastic milk pouches when emptied and use for freezer bags. They are much stronger than the bags you buy.

1053 Save all foil or wax paper margarine wrappers from the quarter-pound squares. Then, when making hamburger patties, use an icecream scoop and scoop out hamburger onto each paper. Fold over and pat to desired thickness. Place on cookie sheet and quick freeze, then store in a plastic bag in the freezer.

1054 Old milk cartons can be filled with water and frozen for use in your picnic hamper.

1055 Save money on ice by filling empty vinegar bottles with water, freezing them and placing them in your cooler.

1056 Styrofoam egg cartons make great bathtub toys.

1057 Save foam egg cartons. They make excellent ice cube trays.

1058 Styrofoam packing chips are good substitutes for the pebbles usually used as the drainage layer in the bottom of plant and flower pots. They permit an easy flow of water, are indestructible and add almost nothing to the weight of the container.

1059 If you always find yourself running out of wax paper, save the liners from cereal boxes. They work well.

1060 Use wax paper bags from cereal boxes to wrap pies for the freezer. Just slip the pies in and seal with tape.

MISCELLANEOUS

MISCELLANEOUS

1061 Styrofoam meat trays are handy to have on hand when you take baking etc. to a social function or other event. They come in several sizes and shapes and can be covered with an appropriate serviette to make them more presentable. Wash and rinse them well and store until required.

1062 Save plastic containers from cottage cheese, yogurt, margarine etc. and use as containers when freezing food.

1063 Wash and save plastic margarine containers for microwave lunches. Throw away or reuse.

1064 Use lids of small plastic margarine tubs to separate hamburger patties when freezing. The patties will not stick together.

1065 Take the lid from an empty four-litre ice-cream container and cut away the lip. You now have a portable cutting board which can be discarded when it becomes worn.

1066 When you can't find a shoehorn, make one out of a gallon plastic container. Just cut to the size you want.

1067 Save all plastic food containers and plastic pails. They come in handy around the house when cleaning brushes, mixing glue etc. After the job, they can then be thrown out.

1068 Save tin coffee containers with plastic lids. They make ideal freezer containers for muffins and cookies.

1069 Label leftovers with a bit of tape on which you can write. Everyone will know at a glance what the containers hold.

1070 When saving items in plastic containers, use a wax crayon to label them. To reuse the container, just wipe the writing off with a dry paper towel.

1071 Make extras of a favorite meal and freeze TV dinner-style portions. Then, on those nights when everyone is on the run, heat in the oven or microwave for a quick meal.

1072 When rubber gloves develop a hole, cut them in strips on the round, both the hand part and fingers, and use as rubber bands.

1073 When rubber gloves get a hole in them, cut off the finger portions. They can be pulled over broom and mop handles to avoid handles marking walls.

1074 If you always wear out one rubber glove, start saving all the good gloves and by turning half of them inside out you will gain a few extra pairs.

1075 Paper towels, used to dry the table after washing it, can be left to dry and used for wiping up messy spills.

1076 Always use lunch bags more than once.

1077 When putting curtains, which may fray easily, on a rod which has sharp ends, wrap ends of the rod with scotch tape.

1078 Place a small piece of cotton in the fingers of rubber gloves to help prevent holes from fingernails.

1079 Sharpen old, dull scissors by cutting through light sandpaper.

1080 When pins become difficult to push through a diaper or fabric, push the pin into a bar of soap.

1081 A slow cooker can be used as a heater for baby bottles or hot compresses, or it can be filled with soup and plugged in by a patient's sickbed.

1082 Place a clean, dry sink mat on the seat of your child's highchair. It will keep him from sliding out of his chair.

1083 To make a highchair guard, cut out a section of an old bathtub mat to fit the seat of your child's highchair. The suction cups will adhere to the seat and prevent the child from slipping.

1084 Baby's car potty will be much simpler to clean if you line it with a plastic bag and plop the works into a Ziploc bag for disposal at the next stop.

1085 Empty facial tissue boxes can be turned upside down and turned into instant garages and houses for bored youngsters to play with.

MISCELLANEOUS

MISCELLANEOUS

1086 Put rubber bands around children's drinking glasses to provide better gripping power and therefore cut down on spills and breakage.

1087 Save large milk cartons and potato chip boxes. Cut off tops and cover with leftover wallpaper to make colorful containers for crayons, markers, games, etc.

1088 Cut off the sides and fronts from empty cereal boxes, tissue boxes, dress boxes etc. and save. These clean, firm surfaces are great for children to use for drawing on. It's much cheaper than buying expensive scrapbooks and drawing paper.

1089 Children can make their own greeting cards by cutting out pictures from magazines and pasting on recipe cards. Add a verse and the card is ready to go.

1090 Candy Lifesavers make wonderful candleholders for a child's birthday cake. They're colorful, edible and inexpensive.

1091 For inexpensive stocking stuffers or party treats, glue last year's calendar pictures onto stiff cardboard then cut into pieces for a jig-saw puzzle.

1092 For inexpensive gifts, crochet carpets, curtains, coverlets and pillow covers for a child's dollhouse.

1093 Plastic trays used for dishes or plastic vegetable bins make pretty and safe storage areas for toys and other children's items.

1094 To make playdough, mix a few drops of food coloring in two cups boiling water. Add ½ cup salt, two tbsp. oil and two tbsp. alum. Knead well and keep in the refrigerator when not in use.

1095 For bubble solution for children's bubble pipes use two tbsp. powdered detergent, one tbsp. glycerin, one cup hot water and a few drops of food coloring. Mix well.

1096 To remove broken off tips left in the crib board from crib pegs, heat sewing needle on the stove element, pierce centre of broken off tip and pull out.

1097 To restore an old deck of playing cards, dust deck with a small amount of talcum powder.

1098 Straighten dented ping pong balls by placing in hot water for 15 minutes.

1099 Tired tennis balls can be given new life by wrapping individually in foil and heating for half an hour in the oven at 200°f to restore bounce. They can be reheated several times.

1100 For a stocking stuffer make a windowsill bouquet with tiny artificial flowers and a pretty perfume bottle.

1101 Here's a stocking stuffer idea. Wrap a bar of colorful, scented soap in nylon netting and tie with ribbon for a fragrant air freshner.

1102 Stumped for stocking stuffers? Plan now for Christmas. For the stamp collector, fill a plastic sandwich bag with used postage stamps and a good magnifying glass.

1103 Cut up used Christmas cards to make labels for next year's Christmas presents.

1104 Instead of store-bought bows for gifts, use pompoms, dried or fabric flowers, measuring spoons, candy canes, balloons, bells, ornaments, barrettes, erasers, combs, etc.

MISCELLANEOUS

MISCELLANEOUS

1105 Instead of commercial wrapping paper, use wallpaper roll ends. They are stronger and often prettier than wrapping paper.

1106 To recycle expensive gift wrap, lightly spritz the wrong side of paper with spray starch, then press with a warm iron.

1107 Towels, scarves and fabric napkins make useful wrapping paper.

1108 Instead of using wrapping paper, wrap wedding gifts in tea towels or bath towels. Wrap baby gifts in receiving blankets. T-shirts, scarves, socks and cloth napkins can also be used as gift wrap. Decorate packages with hair ribbons, balloons, dried flowers etc.

1109 Use scrap material or old sheets, towels etc. to make gift bags. Cut material into the size you need, sew a one-inch seam for the drawstring and sew bag together.

1110 Arrange painted picture frames over newly wallpapered walls for inexpensive, yet effective decorating.

1111 Use leftover wallpaper for shelf paper and drawer liners.

1112 Save postcards and special occasion cards and laminate them. Use to line shelves and drawers.

1113 Squeeze a new roll of toilet tissue before installing. This will prevent waste because it won't roll excessively.

1114 Toilet tissue is much cheaper and goes a lot further than facial tissue. Also, you can use more or less as needed.

1115 When you receive junk mail which includes return envelopes, use the envelopes to store small items such as seeds, pictures etc.

1116 Use the backs of business envelopes and the unwritten side of circulars for writing grocery lists, notes to children, etc.

1117 When mailing a get-well card to someone in hospital, use the patient's return address rather than your own. In this way, should the person have been released from hospital, he is assured of getting the card.

1118 Don't seal or write on the envelope if you are delivering a greeting card in person. The envelope can be reused to mail a letter.

1119 Reuse large-size envelopes that you receive in the mail. Glue paper over old address to readdress.

1120 Use the clean, unused side of paper to send faxes.

1121 Drop off entry forms or pay bills when you are in the area of the business. When leaving the house always think, is there anything I can pay on the way? Stamps add up; it just takes a minute, when in the area, to run in and pay a bill.

1122 If your stamps and envelopes are stuck together, place them in the freezer for an hour or so. Then you should be able to spread the stuck part easily with a knife without damaging the glue.

1123 The perforated salvage edges on postage stamp sheets make good jar labels for home preserves.

1124 If stamps have stuck together, put them in the freezer for a while. They will come apart easily without harming the glue.

1125 Dampen the string before tying a parcel. It will not slip and, as it dries, it shrinks and keeps tight.

MISCELLANEOUS

MISCELLANEOUS

1126 To soften the tip of a felt-tipped marking pen which has hardened after being left uncovered for a long time, place a few drops of spot remover in a dish and work the tip around in it. When soft, wipe tip.

1127 To keep track of addresses, use 3x5 cards and make out new ones when addresses change.

1128 To keep addresses handy for your personal correspondence, cut or tear return address label off letters and tape on the back cardboard of your current writing pad. Remove to new pad each time one is started. They are always at your fingertips when writing letters.

1129 Card file — Store important information on separate cards. Use an extra recipe box, file alphabetically, and print headings in large letters. This saves a lot of searching time. I save bike serial numbers, home address lot block, plan numbers, company addresses. Cards can be cut from lightweight cardboard from packages of panty hose, etc.

1130 Use a variety of cereal, detergent and pet food boxes to make magazine, bill, map, recipe and craft instruction files. Just cut off the tops of the boxes on an angle, tape boxes together in sets and cover them with wrapping paper or wallpaper.

1131 Make copies of your credit cards in case they are misplaced or stolen.

1132 When going away on holiday, store important papers in the refrigerator or freezer. In case of fire, the papers will be safe.

1133 When unable to obtain typewriter ribbon to fit your typewriter, save the cans from the old ribbons and rewind it with any available new ribbon.

1134 Never throw out unwanted "this or that." Place in a box marked garage sale and store until spring. Someone will make you an offer at your next sale.

1135 Form a video rental "co-op" where you have friends over when you rent a video and they have you over when they rent one. Both families save money.

1136 Make moving day easier for you and the movers. Use colored markers and designate one specific color for each room of the house. The movers will be able to carry your boxes to the correct rooms without needing constant assistance.

1137 If arthritis is making it difficult to grasp a pen, push the pen through a small rubber ball.

1138 To help an invalid or person of limited mobility, buy a pair of barbecue tongs. They are ideal for retrieving articles which are out of reach.

1139 Instead of buying special trays to give someone breakfast in bed, use a muffin tin. It neatly fits glasses, cups and individual portions of food.

1140 If a screw tends to come out of your eyeglasses, apply clear nail polish over it.

1141 A valuable tool in the kitchen is a nutcracker. It's ideal to use for loosening bottle tops and jar lids.

1142 To open a tightly sealed jar, wrap a rubber tourniquet around lid and it will open easily.

1143 A clothespin makes a great clip for potato chip bags.

MISCELLANEOUS

MISCELLANEOUS

1144 When you get a set of measuring spoons, undo the wire holding them together and leave the spoons standing loose in a cup or glass. This way, you need only wash the spoon used instead of the whole set.

1145 Stacked tumblers often stick together and are difficult to separate. To avoid this, drop a toothpick into the bottom of the tumbler before inserting the next one. The toothpick will support the upper tumbler and keep it from sticking in place.

1146 If kitchen glasses are stuck together, fill the top glass with cold water and dip the bottom glass in hot water.

1147 When two glasses or bowls are stuck together, put a few ice cubes in the top one and set the bottom one in hot water. Let stand a few minutes and they'll come apart easily.

1148 If the plastic pump supplied with commercial window cleaner, hand cream etc. doesn't reach the bottom of the bottle, you can extend the tube with waterproof adhesive tape.

1149 To make old plastic flowers look like new, spray with hairspray.

1150 Soak a new broom in hot, heavily salted water to give it a longer life.

1151 Keep extra shower hooks in sewing basket to hold pins.

1152 Shower hooks can be used as key chains.

1153 Set your alarm clock on a tin plate. It will be heard.

1154 When eating outside, staple the tablecloth at each corner, so the wind can't take it.

1155 When camping, take a roll of clear plastic and a stapler. When the winds blow, just fasten the plastic on trees around the campsite.

1156 If your plan to eat in restaurants while travelling, make lunch your main meal of the day. Many places charge more for the same meal at night.

1157 Take an old barbecue grill with you when camping. It can be used on any barbecue in any campground and can always be kept clean.

1158 Only grocery shop once a week — you'll save money by buying less.

1159 Never grocery shop on a Monday morning when stock is depleted or anemic.

1160 Always eat before you go grocery shopping. You'll buy less.

1161 Always shop with a grocery list.

1162 Grocery shop alone — leave the kids with a sitter and never take your husband.

1163 Take a calculator when shopping and calculate the cost per unit.

1164 Use manufacturers' coupons, but only for foods which you would normally buy.

1165 Record all expenditures. This slows down spending and people find out exactly where their hard-earned dollars are going.

1166 Check foods on the lowest shelves at the grocery store. They are usually less expensive.

MISCELLANEOUS

1167 Buy groceries on sale and always buy more than one of the sale items. This way you can stock up on groceries without paying regular price.

1168 Buy as many household items and groceries by the case as possible.

1169 Buy two pairs of the same color socks — when one sock wears out, you always have two more which match.

1170 A candle will fit most candlesticks if dipped in hot water first.

1171 Chill candles in the refrigerator 24 hours before using them. They will burn evenly and won't drip.

1172 Keep two or three candles in the refrigerator freezer. If there is a power failure, they are easy to find.

1173 To prevent a candle from dripping, place a little salt around the top of the candle before lighting.

1174 Crumbled bay leaves, placed in a cupboard, will discourage insects.

1175 To get rid of cockroaches in your home or garage, wash off shelves and the spaces behind the stove and refrigerator. Sprinkle clean areas with baking soda. When the roaches make contact with the baking soda, they dry up.

1176 Make your own moth repellent by mixing four oz. of rosemary, four oz. of mint leaves, two oz. of thyme, one tbsp. ground cloves and one tsp. of ground orris root. Let it age for several weeks.

1177 Place cucumber peels on the kitchen windowsill to keep ants out.

1178 Salt or red pepper sprinkled on counters and across doors and windowsills is a barrier for ants.

1179 Scatter a package of mothballs under your cottage or cabin to keep mice and skunks away.

1180 If you are camping in bear country and you want the bears to stay away, scatter some moth balls around your tent area.

1181 Rinse out empty milk carton and use as mini garbage container by the sink.

1182 Use a plastic grocery bag, inserted in a plastic wastebasket to collect garbage under the sink. When the bag is full, use the handles of the grocery bag to tie a firm knot in the bag, then place in your outdoor garbage can.

1183 Keep plastic grocery bags, which are to be used as garbage bags in empty facial tissue boxes. It keeps them tidy.

1184 Used, four-quart milk bags are great for lining the bathroom garbage bin.

1185 To prevent your garbage from filling up so quickly, after emptying a tin can, open the opposite end and flatten the can before throwing away.

1186 To have garbage bags handy, put some of them in garbage pail under the garbage bag in use.

1187 Farm tip: Get paper bags for groceries and recycle as garbage bags. Paper bags help burn the garbage more completely.

1188 Throw a few mothballs into the garbage can to neutralize odors and keep out insects.

MISCELLANEOUS

MISCELLANEOUS

1189 Put a few capfuls of Pinesol into bagged garbage to keep cats and dogs away.

1190 Save water from cooked vegetables to mix with your dog's dry food. It will add extra flavor and vitamins.

1191 Attach a rubber suction cup to the bottom of your pet's dish to keep it from sliding while the pet eats.

1192 If your dog knocks over his food dish when eating, anchor a one-gallon pail to the ground by driving spikes through it. If you want to be able to clean it or cut grass around it, buy a tube-cake pan and drop it over a stake driven into the ground.

1193 Store big bags of dry dog food in a clean garbage can with a lid.

1194 Brewer's yeast rubbed on your dog's coat prevents fleas.

1195 Make a portable dog anchor by tying his leash around an old tire and putting a few bricks inside.

1196 If the kids are begging for a dog, have them walk the neighbor's for a month.

1197 Rub petroleum jelly on the hinges and door knobs before you start to paint a door. If you get paint on them, they will wipe off easy.

1198 To keep white paint from yellowing, add 10 drops of black paint to each quart of white.

1199 When painting ceilings, cut a child's rubber ball in half and put your paint brush in one of the halves to catch the drips.

1200 An old pair of swimming goggles will protect your eyes from paint splatters and drips when painting ceilings.

1201 When painting, protect your hands and face with moisturizer. Cleanup will be easier and the moisturizer will prevent paint from seeping into the pores.

1202 Before starting to paint with enamel paint, lightly coat your hands and underneath your fingernails with any name brand hand cleaner. After the painting is finished, your hands will be easy to clean.

1203 Line your paint tray with aluminum foil. When it's time to clean up, just roll up the foil and throw away.

1204 To stop paint from dripping, punch a few holes in the rim of the paint can. When the brush is wiped against the edge, the paint flows back into the can. The lid covers the holes so the paint won't dry out.

1205 To remove lumps from paint: Cut a piece of screen to fit the inside of the paint can. Set it on top of the paint and let it float down to the bottom of the can. It will take all the lumps with it, trapping them at the bottom of the can.

1206 When painting trim around windows, doorways etc. try using stiff paper to cover the area you don't want painted. (An old phone book cover works well.) Slide paper along as you paint. It's much faster and more economical than using masking tape. Works well with either a roller or brush.

1207 When painting a room, dip a small card into the paint so that you have the exact color with you and can match accessories in stores.

1208 When painting inside corners, trim the paint brush bristles to a V to save strokes and spread paint more evenly.

HANDY PERSON TIPS

HANDY PERSON TIPS

1209 Before pouring paint from a can, cover the rim with masking tape. After pouring, remove the tape — the rim will be clean and the cover will fit tightly.

1210 When you poke a paint brush into corners or allow it to rest on the bottom of the paint can, the bristles curl and stray. To straigthen natural bristles (not synthetics), try wrapping the brush in a couple of thicknesses of damp cloth and press gently with an iron. The steam and cloth binding do the job. Only light pressure is needed. Let the bristles cool before you unwrap the brush.

1211 When painting old woodwork, fill in the holes or cracks with a mixture of flour and some of the paint you are using. It hardens like cement and matches perfectly.

1212 When painting stairs, paint every other step first. When these are dry, paint the rest.

1213 To avoid cleaning paint brushes and rollers if you intend to use the same color later, or if you do not have time to clean immediately, place the brushes and rollers in a plastic bag, tie shut and place in the freezer. They will keep for several days without drying up.

1214 Protect hands from paint solvent by putting the brush and solvent into a strong plastic bag. With hands outside the bag, work the solvent into the brush through the plastic.

1215 After cleaning your paint brush, a few drops of oil worked into the bristles will leave the brush soft and ready to use.

1216 To clean paint rollers, fill an empty one-quart milk carton with solvent, put the roller inside and crimp the ends shut. Give the carton a few shakes, then let sit for a couple of hours.

1217 Simmer hardened paint brushes in full-strength vinegar. Remove the softened paint with a wire comb or brush.

1218 To remove oil or enamel paint from your hands, rub on paste floor wax and then wash with plenty of soap and warm water. There is no odor and it's easier on the skin than paint remover.

1219 In time, a partly used can of paint will develop a skin on top. To prevent this, cut waxpaper the size of the can and drop it in.

1220 To save partial cans of leftover paint, fill the airspace with a lightly inflated balloon before pressing on the lid.

1221 A coat of penetrating stain applied to a smooth wood surface may last only three or four years, but a second application after the wood has weathered will last as long as 10.

1222 To give bathroom fixtures a new look, paint with an epoxy paint, sold especially for that purpose.

1223 Never stir varnish. It has no color pigments which need blending and stirring will create air bubbles which can ruin a smooth finish.

1224 To frost a bathroom or garage window, make a solution of one cup of beer to four tbsp. Epsom salts and paint on the window. It washes off when you want a clear pane again.

1225 If you have a small hole in your wall (after moving pictures etc.) take a wax crayon as near the color of your wall as possible. Rub the hole with the crayon, polish with a dry cloth and the hole is invisible.

1226 Clean out old nail polish bottles and fill with 'touch-up' paint for scuffs and scratches that may occur on your walls.

1227 When hanging pictures on plaster walls, put a small piece of adhesive tape where the nail is to go in. Drive the nail through the tape. This helps prevent the plaster from cracking.

HANDY PERSON TIPS

HANDY PERSON TIPS

1228 When drilling a hole in any kind of wall, take an envelope, crease the edges to hold it open, then fasten it to the wall just under where you are drilling. It keeps a great deal of mess from hitting the floor and makes clean-up easier.

1229 After wallpapering or painting, write the amount under a light-switch plate and you'll always know how much wallpaper or paint you need for that room.

1230 To remove old wallpaper, first pull off as much as you can, then soak the remaining with Fleecy. It will peel off easily.

1231 Before wallpapering a wall, apply a coat of clear varnish to any grease spots. This will prevent the grease from soaking through the new paper.

1232 Instead of applying wallpaper with a sponge, dip a paint roller in the solution, squeeze slightly to prevent dripping and roll it over 20-30 sq. feet at a time.

1233 Buy stair carpeting a little longer than needed. When it shows signs of wear it can be shifted downward to delay replacement.

1234 To avoid wearing out spots on heavy traffic areas, use extra pieces of material cut out of the same material as the rug or linoleum.

1235 If your kitchen cupboards have worn out or if there are scuff marks around the handles, remove handles and glue on tiles to cover the scuffs. Replace handles over the tiles. This adds an interesting color accent and saves replacing or refinishing the doors.

1236 When a drain is clogged with grease, pour a cup of salt and a cup of baking soda into the drain, followed by a kettle of boiling water.

1237 If your water taps have a tendency to freeze during a cold spell, leave your taps on slightly. Running water will not freeze.

1238 Frozen water pipes can safely and easily be thawed out by using an ordinary hair dryer nozzle directed at the frozen pipe.

1239 To tighten cane-bottomed chairs, turn them upside down and liberally apply hot water to the underside. Dry the chairs in the sun.

1240 When sanding or refinishing, cover your hand with an old nylon stocking. Glide your hand over the surface to be redone. Any rough areas will snag the stocking where more sanding needs to be done.

1241 To restore odor to an old cedar chest or closet, sandpaper lightly. This reopens pores in the wood to restore breathing.

1242 Spring-type clothespins are useful as clamps to hold lightweight glued materials together.

1243 To find a wall stud, hold a pocket compass level with the floor and at a right angle to the wall. Slowly move it along the surface of the wall. Movement of the compass will indicate the presence of nails and reveal stud location.

1244 You always have a measuring tape in your pocket — a dollar bill is exactly six inches long and just short of three inches wide.

1245 Use nonstick vegetable spray to lubricate squeaky hinges and sticky locks.

1246 Loosen rusted nuts or bolts with a few drops of ammonia or peroxide.

HANDY PERSON TIPS

1247 Stop drawers from sticking by running a candle along the tops.

1248 To help remove stubborn nuts and bolts, pour on some cola soft drink.

1249 You can retrieve a broken key by putting some strong metal adhesive on the handle and holding it to the part stuck in the lock. Hold it there until the glue has set. When it holds, pull out the key. Don't use the key again.

1250 Four or five mothballs in your toolbox will keep the tools from rusting.

1251 A piece of chalk or charcoal in your toolbox will attract moisture and keep your tools from rusting.

1252 Save your old nuts, bolts and washers. They make excellent sinkers for your fishing line.

1253 Use discarded milk cartons, with the tops cut off, to store items in the workshop. Great for nails, screws etc.

1254 If one of your saucepan lids is missing a knob, put a screw through the hole with the point upwards and push a cork down onto it.

1255 To store a handsaw safely, cover the teeth with a split length of old garden hose.

1256 To sharpen scissors, fold a piece of aluminum foil three times, then cut through it several times with your scissors.

1257 Electrical cords from kitchen appliances are easy to find when stored in cardboard tubes from disposable towels. Color code the end of the tube if you have more than one in a drawer.

1258 Tuck electric appliance cords and extension cords into toilet tissue tubes, labelling each by length and by which cord fits which appliance.

1259 To keep cords of curling irons and blow dryers together in a drawer, use ponytail holders.

1260 To remove broken lightbulbs with ease, put switch into off position, then push a raw potato into the base and twist the broken bulb out.

1261 To get a broken lightbulb out of the socket, turn the switch off, then stick a soft bar of soap into the jagged edges of glass and use the soap as a handle to unscrew it easily and safely.

1262 If your flashlight batteries are getting weak while on a camping trip and you cannot replace them immediately, set them in the bright sunlight during the day and they will be temporarily rejuvenated.

1263 The charcoal in a rangehood filter can be recharged by placing it in a 450-degree oven for 30 minutes after cleaning the metal frame.

1264 When mailing fragile items, pack the excess space in the box with popped popcorn to insulate the package against damage/breakage.

1265 To allow sliding windows or drawers to move easier, use a bar of soap to grease tracks or runners.

1266 When a pin or needle won't penetrate an article, rub pin or needle in your hair and try again.

1267 Why climb a ladder? Use binoculars to get a closer look.

1268 Your ladder won't sink into soft earth if you place each leg into an empty coffee can or paint can.

HANDY PERSON TIPS

1269 A discarded fan belt from the car makes an ideal gutter-cleaning tool. Being flexible, yet firm, this belt is easily formed to shape the bottom of the gutter which enables muck and leaves to be scraped out without scratching the paint inside the gutter.

1270 Use old or leftover linoleum to cover seats and tops of picnic tables.

1271 Small holes in window screens can be repaired by dabbing the hole with successive layers of clear nail polish.

1272 Put an extra house key in a water-tight container or plastic bag and store outside the house in the flower bed, under a rock etc. so you will never be locked out.

1273 Use extra-large plastic garbage bags as inexpensive protective covers for folding lawn furniture. This allows furniture to be stored outdoors without damage.

1274 Snow will slide off a shovel which has been sprayed with furniture polish or vegetable oil.

1275 Rub your snow shovel with parawax or candle wax before using. Even wet snow will slide off without buildup, keeping the shovel light and easy to manoeuvre.

1276 Use your fertilizer spreader to scatter sand on icy walkways.

1277 To remove dangerous ice off your steps, sprinkle with salt.

1278 Kitty litter can be used to de-ice your sidewalks and steps.

1279 Fireplace Starters or Lighters: Save the lint from your dryer and paper egg cartons (not styrofoam). Cut egg cartons into individual cups and fill cups with lint. Melt wax (from old candle stubs) and pour some over the lint. When lighting the fireplace use these, place them under the kindling in the fireplace. They are slow burning and do a great job in lighting the fire.

1280 Dried orange and grapefruit peels and rind make good fuel in a fireplace and give off a lovely aroma as they burn.

1281 Throw salt on fireplace logs once a month to prevent soot in the fireplace.

1282 To prevent your fireplace from smoking, raise the fire grate by placing bricks under the legs.

1283 Save your Nabob coffee bags to burn in the fireplace. Roll up tightly and then watch the varicolored flames when the bags are burned.

1284 To add a little color to your campfire, soak pinecones in a solution of ½ gallon water and ½ pound Borax. When dry, they burn a vivid green.

1285 To make your Christmas tree last longer, add sugar to the water.

1286 To preserve your Christmas tree longer, add Pinesol to the water.

1287 To fireproof the Christmas tree, mix eight oz. boracic acid in one gallon of water. Spray mixture over tree and let dry.

1288 To clean automobile chrome, rub with dampened aluminum foil.

1289 Add one cup of kerosene to the wash water when washing the car. Wipe well with a soft cloth — no rinsing is necessary. This will prevent rust and water will actually bead on the car during a rainfall.

1290 Wash your car with liquid dishwashing detergent. It won't scratch the surface.

HANDY PERSON TIPS

HANDY PERSON TIPS

1291   Use dry baking soda on a damp cloth to clean the bugs off the car windshield.

1292   Windshield wipers smearing? Clean the windshield and wiper blade with rubbing alcohol.

1293   Make your own windshield washer fluid by combining one quart rubbing alcohol, one cup water and two Tblsp. liquid detergent.

1294   Use steel wool pads on your tire white side walls to keep them new looking.

1295   Keep open cans of motor oil clean by sealing them with the plastic lids from one-pound tins of coffee.

1296   A sheet of fabric softener under your car seat will keep the car smelling fresh.

1297   To clean corrosion from battery posts, make a paste of baking soda and water (paste should be thickness of cream). Brush on posts, leave for 10 minutes and brush off with water. Wipe dry with a rag. This leaves the posts and battery clean.

1298   Before leaving on holidays or a weekend trip in the summer, spray the front of your car with cooking oil (such as Pam). This will keep the bugs from sticking to the grill. Those that do will wash off with ease.

1299 Place moth balls in car trunk and interior if you're going to park your vehicle for several months. Mice will not take up occupancy.

1300 Run your car air-conditioner five minutes weekly during the winter months to keep it in good condition.

1301 Prevent car doors from freezing by wiping the rubber gaskets with vegetable oil to seal out water.

1302 If your car door locks freeze, use your hairdryer to thaw them out.

1303 If door locks are frozen and a hairdryer is not available, heat the key with a lighter or match.

1304 To avoid having your car extension cord stolen, buy a somewhat longer cord, plug it in and, with the extra length, loop it and put it inside the door and close it. An alternative is to drive the front wheel over the cord.

1305 Your car block heater may be plugged in but the current may not be getting through. To make certain it is, wire in an inexpensive circuit test into the receptacle end of the heater cord. When you see the glow, you know the current is getting through.

1306 Be prepared for winter driving by purchasing a strip of expanded metal about eight inches wide and 24 inches long. (This is a diamond-patterned screen that can be purchased at most tin smith shops.) When placed under the wheels of your vehicle, it can get you out of most spots.

1307 If your car is stuck in snow, your floor mats or an old carpet, stored in the trunk, can be placed under the rear wheels for traction.

1308 Save old milk cartons and fill with sand to carry in your car in case you get stuck in the snow.

1309 Fill old milk cartons with old melted candles and/or parawax, insert a wick and keep in the trunk of your car in case of winter emergency.

HANDY PERSON TIPS

1310 When travelling in the winter be prepared. Carry in your trunk a couple of plastic pails of dry sand, one small shovel, sleeping bags, a well-charged flashlight, outdoor extension cord and a couple of pairs of heavy wool socks (you can always use socks on your hands but it is difficult to put gloves on your feet). Always make certain that your gas tank is above the half-full mark.

1311 Preserve your garage floor, particularly in the winter, by placing carpet remnants on the area where the tires come in contact with the floor.

1312 To remove grease and oil stains from concrete, first scrape off as much of the stain as possible with a putty knife. Wet down the stains and sprinkle on TSP crystals (Trisodium Phosphate Crystals which can be purchased from most hardware stores). As the crystals dissolve, use a bristle brush and work on the stain for 15-20 minutes. Add a little more TSP and brush the spot vigorously. Mop up stain with clean water.

1313 Here are ways to remove oil stains on your driveway. For fresh stains, sprinkle kitty litter, grind in with your foot, let it absorb the oil, then sweep up. For older stains, use Spray N Wash, let stand approximately five minutes, then sprinkle on laundry detergent, scrub with stiff broom, then hose down. For really tough stains, use oven spray, let set and rinse with clear water.

DONORS

Aldridge, Irene, Regina
Ames, Stewart, Yorkton
Amos, Maxine, Oxbow
Anwender, Amelia, Regina
Avery, Donna, Oxbow
Bague, Elvira, Regina
Baker, Denise, Raymore
Baker, E., Broadview
Bakken, Beulah, Balgonie
Bakkel, Marg, Shaunavon
Baliko, Joan, Regina
Bandet, Roland, Regina
Barkman, Mary, Regina
Barton, Darlene, Regina
Beattie, Joy, Swift Current
Bechdoldt, Lynne, Regina
Becker, Mrs. O., Rocanville
Beckstead, Eleanor, Creelman
Behr, R., Estevan
Beke, Della Rose, Regina
Belbeck, Bernice, Rockglen
Belisle, Julie, Wauchope
Bencharski, Gwen, Elfros
Bengert, Marla, Regina
Benz, Brian, Regina
Benz, Marilyn, Regina
Berkes, Winnifred, Whitewood
Berling, Doreen, Regina
Berube, Sam, Regina
Best, Mrs. B., Balgonie
Billingsley, Mrs. D., Regina
Billingsley, Jess, Regina
Bilan, Flo, Preeceville
Bilan, H., Preeceville
Bissett, Joan, Regina
Biyak, Kathy, Regina
Blackwood, Lillian, Regina
Blancher, Janet, Regina
Bleachley, Gordon, Pilot Butte
Bleackley, B., Swift Current
Blumhagen, Jean, Regina
Boa, Mae, Regina
Bodnarchuk, Sonya, Canora
Beochler, Sandra, Regina
Bogdan, Louise, Qu'Appelle
Bolton, Linda, Ceylon
Bonneau, Paul L., Gravelbourg
Boyd, Ruth, Regina
Braumberger, Michelle, McLean
Bray, Teresa, McLean
Brentnell, E.R., Belle Plaine
Bressler, Norma, Regina
Brewer, Tom, Regina
Broad, Shirley, Melville
Bruener, Rudy, White City
Buckner, Gloria, Beaubier
Budd, Marrella, Regina

Bulych, Lydia, Ituna
Burns, Sue, Regina
Burr, Wendy, Weyburn
Cameron, Dixie, Carievale
Campbell, Agnes, Regina
Campbell, D.H. Pitt Meadow, B.C.
Carlson-Lewis, Cheryl, Rocanville
Carr, Kay, Shaunavon
Caswell, Helen, Moose Jaw
Cave, Kathleen, Shaunavon
Cave, Mrs. W., Regina
Celentano, Sandra, Regina
Chase, Marilyn M.D., Moose Jaw
Chatterton, Robyn, Wolseley
Chester, Wanda, Broadview
Chopik, Doris, Regina
Chopty, Marlene, Preeceville
Christenson, Jean, Estevan
Clairmont, L., Esterhazy
Clark, Ms. Rae, Maple Clark
Clarke, Mrs. A., Avonlea
Clarke, Kathleen, Wolseley
Clarkson, Lois, Redvers
Clemence, Leslie, Regina
Cole, Marg, Regina
Colton, Lily E., Manor
Cook, Bryan, Esterhazy
Cooley, Caron, Esterhazy
Cooney, Margaret, Glen Ewen
Costea, Patricia, Regina
Costron, Judy, Regina
Couprie, Rose, Regina
Crawford, L., Pilot Butte
Cross, Sally, Regina
Culbertson, P., Welwyn
Curtis, Kathie, Lumsden
Curtis, Suzanne, Wolseley
Dahl, Mrs. Muriel, Regina
Dartige, Diane, Whitewood
Deaust, Dianne, Regina
Deadlock, Anna, Estevan
Delsnider, Ken, Regina
Demchuk, Anne, Regina
Dereninsky, Allan, Saskatoon
Dereninsky, Elaine, Regina
Dereniwsky, Kevin, Saskatoon
Dereniwsky, Larry, Esterhazy
Derksen, Clara, Swift Current
Dewar, Trudy, Regina
Dewhurst, Laurie, Regina
Dickin, Muriel, Manor
Digney, Eva, Raymore
Dillistone, Gareth, Regina
Dillistone, Patricia, Regina
Dmyterko, Diane, Regina
Dorais, Marian, Regina
Doreau, Greg, Regina

Dukart, Mrs. Jean, Estevan
Dumonceaux, Harvey, Kipling
Dunger, Leona, Regina
Dunn, Nancy, Moose Jaw
Dunn, Eve, Regina
Dusterbeck, Jo, Regina
Dwyer, Leona, Regina
Eagles, Barbara A., Regina
Eaket, Agnes, Kenosee
Eberle, Mrs. E., Regina
Eberle, Marlene, Regina
Eddy, Kathleen, Foam Lake
Edwards, John, Regina
Elchuk, Darlene, Regina
Ellefson, Anne, Regina
Entner, Heather, Regina
Erfle, Anita, Regina
Erhardt, Lenore, Strasbourg
Erickson, Judi, Radville
Erickson, Peggy, Strasbourg
Evelt, Rosemarie, Regina
Fahlman, Peggy, Regina
Faller, Ruth, Southey
Farrell, Dianna, Regina
Fazakas, Lorrie, Cupar
Fee, D., Regina
Finch, Cora, Regina
Fisher, Helen, Moose Jaw
Fisher, Norma, Regina
Flaman, Ruby, Regina
Floen, Mrs. E., Oxbow
Fodey, Dolores, Regina
Folk, N., Regina
Foord, Janet, Macoun
Ford, Rose, Central Butte
Francis, Alma, Regina
Fraser, Barb, Regina
Fraser, David, Regina
Froehlich, Bud, Marquis
Froehlich, Dora, Marquis
Froehlich, Lois, Regina
Fuchs, Carolyn, Regina
Fulcher, Mrs. Orlean, Regina
Galbiati, Vici, Regina
Galenzoski, Lillian, Balgonie
Ganje, Mrs. Bella, Estevan
Ganshorn, Barb, Regina
Garner, Gloria, Arcola
Gibbens, Myrna, Regina
Gibbons, Donna, Weyburn
Gibbs, Karen, Regina
Gibson, Josephine, Regina
Gibson, Mrs. Lois, Regina
Ginter, Marion, Swift Current
Glaspey, Mrs. James, Oxbow
Glennie, Sheila, Wadena
Goeres, Isabel, Weyburn

Gorniak, Ev, Regina
Gorrill, Mrs. Brenda, Regina
Gosselin, Marion, Regina
Gottselig, Marie, Balgonie
Grady, Barbara, Estevan
Grant, Mrs. Barbara, Estevan
Green, Christine, Craven
Greggain, Lorna, Regina
Gress, Matt, Regina
Gress, Joan, Regina
Groff, Glenn, Regina
Gutfriend, Monica, Regina
Hack, Mrs. G., Regina
Hack, H., Regina
Hackewich, Mary, Regina
Hala, Gertrude, Regina
Hammett, Cheryl, Regina
Handy, Sharon, Calgary, Alta.
Harker, Kay, Regina
Harty, Brenda, Regina
Harper, Irene, Redvers
Hastings, Edith A., Regina Beach
Hawryluk, Barbara, Kamsack
Haywood, Bernie, Regina
Heath, Heather, Regina
Hehn, Mrs. Alice, Regina
Heidinger, Helen, Arcola
Heibein, Eileen, Zehner
Heilman, Jane, Moose Jaw
Heisler, Helen, Regina
Henderson, Teresa, Gainsborough
Herperger, Cheryl, Regina
Hill, Scott, Pangman
Hilt, Merelyn, Regina
Himmelspeck, Neil, Regina
Hodgson, Lill, Regina
Hotcher, Irene, Regina
Hrywkiw, Brenda, Langenburg
Huber, Eunice, Lipton
Hugel, Caroline, Regina
Hutchen, Irene, Regina
Irwin, Mary, Estevan
James, Beverly, Swift Current
Janowski, Jean, Weyburn
Jawoski, Jean, Regina
Jewsbury, Velma, Regina
Johnson, A.D., Regina
Johnson, Mrs. E.M., Regina
Johnson, Sheila, Gainsborough
Jolly, Mrs. Lois, Regina
Jones, Irene M., Edgeley
Jones, Patricia, Weyburn
Jones, Sharon, Weyburn
Josin, Mrs. Freda, Regina
Kahon, Shirley, Regina
Kalynuk, Mrs. G., Canora
Kambeitz, Gailene, Regina

Karlonas, Ida-Mae, Balgonie
Kaytor, Joan, Regina
Keene, Mrs. Agnes, Regina
Kegel, Georgina, Pilot Butte
Kelln, Emma, Semans
Kemery, Noreen, Kipling
Kennedy, Ann, Newport
Kennedy, Ann Marie, Regina
Kennedy, Freda, McLean
Kipes, Helena, Roblin, Man.
Kippan, Anna, Regina
Kirby, Betty, Gainsborough
Klemp, Edith, Pense
Kness, Kathy, Regina
Knibbs, Mrs. Susan, Carnduff
Knoblauch, Vi, Griffin
Konoff, Mrs. Bunny, Regina
Konoff, Mrs. Mariann, Regina
Krause, Mrs. J., Regina
Krentz, Caroline D., Regina
Krueger, Glenn, Shaunavon
Krushkowski, Anne, Kamsack
Kunz, Betty, Regina
Kuyek, Dale, Regina
Laing, Alma, Swift Current
Laing, George, Swift Current
Lambord, Marie, Estevan
Lang, Dorothy, Chamberlain
Langenegger, Pat, McLean
Langenegger, Steve, McLean
Langelotz, Sighilde, Regina
Lanigan, R.M., Regina
Lapiere, Donna, Regina
Lareau, Lill, Regina
Laurans, Irene, Regina
Lawrence, Mrs. Lily, Regina
Leggett, Mrs. R.I., Kipling
Lehmann, Katherine, Regina
Leier, Kathie, Regina
Lepoudre, Faith, Balgonie
Levenick, Elsie, Regina
Lewko, Kathy, Regina
Linnell, Jean, Summerberry
Linnell, Joe, Summerberry
Liski, G., Regina
Longworth, Darlene, Regina
Loos, Ron, Yellow Grass
Lott, Shirley, Regina
Love, Mrs. Jean, Moose Jaw
Lussier, Margaret, Regina
Lynch, Mary, Moose Jaw
Macknak, Georgina, Regina
Macri, Mrs. Frank, Regina
MacLean, Marion, Melville
Mang, Mrs. Joyce, Pense
Mann, Eleanor, Grenfell
Manz, T., Regina

Marion, Merle, Davidson
Marshall, Gertrude, Melville
Mayes, Eleanor, Regina
McAllister, Diane, Maple Creek
McClelland, Elsie, Regina
McGrath, Delia, Regina
McGregor, Nell, Central Butte
McGillicky, Julie Ann, Coronach
McLafferty, Norma, Moose Jaw
McLashen, Helen, Yorkton
McNab, Valerie, Langbank
Melle, Deb, Minton
Merriman, Doris, Regina
Metereo, Mrs. Jeannie, Regina
Miller, J., Estevan
Miller, Robert, Regina
Miller, Rose, Estevan
Mildenberger, Les, Sedley
Mildenberger, Sally, Sedley
Minto, Garth, Regina
Minto, Sharlene, Regina
Mitchell, Douglas, Kamsack
Monroe, Beverly, Regina
Monteyne, Darlene, Estevan
Montgomery, Jean, Morse
Morris, Eileen, Gravelbourg
Morton, Laura, Kisbey
Moskal, Eva, Veregin
Mozylisky, Tony, Regina
Munro, Joyce, Swift Current
Mula, Sharon, Regina
Murdoch, Mrs. Joyce, Shaunavon
Murray, M., Regina
Murray, Patsy D., Regina
Nehn, Mrs. Alice, Regina
Nelson, Mrs. Arlene, Wilcox
Nelson, Nancy, Regina
Nelson, Mrs. Rose, Stockholm
Nerby, Helen E., Indian Head
Nichol, Elizabeth, Swift Current
Noess, Edith, Assiniboia
Nording, Mrs. Carolyn, Regina
Norman, B., Regina
Oberndorfer, Karl, Regina
Ohashi, Mrs. A., Regina
Oleksinski, Mrs. E., Regina
Olson, Mrs. P., Sturgis
Olson, Russell, Weyburn
Orban, Luana, Regina
Orser, Christina, Regina
Orthner, Viola, Regina
Osolinski, Stan, Yorkton
Pacholka, Adeline, Yorkton
Parker, Robert, Regina
Parker, Vic, Regina
Pask, Jean, Esterhazy
Paterson, Donna, Edenwold

Pattison, Bonnie, Regina
Peart, Betty Ann, Regina
Peart, Christine, Regina
Peel, Betty Ann, Regina
Pepin, Sharon, Regina
Perepiolkin, Fred, Swift Current
Perepiolkin, Susan, Swift Current
Perepiolkin, Winnie, Swift Current
Perkins, A. Kay, Rouleau
Peterson, Kathy, Regina
Peterson, Patti, Regina
Pickering, Shirley, Weyburn
Piluk, Mary Jane, Estevan
Pinkering, P., Earl Grey
Popowich, Mary, Wynyard
Powley, J.C., Regina
Powley, Mrs. L., Regina
Powell, Bernice D., Yorkton
Powchuck, Mrs. Peter, Grenfell
Powchuck, Peter, Grenfell
Predy, Ruth, Canora
Preikchat, Rose, White City
Priddell, Shirley, Qu'Appelle
Pritchard, D., Regina
Procyk, Caroline, Montmartre
Procyk, Steven, Montmartre
Procyk, Wanda, Montmartre
Prosofsky, Tracey, Regina
Purdy, Elaine, Tantallon
Purvis, Donna, Carlyle
Rathgeber, Marie, Melville
Reed, Richard, Craven
Reed, Verna, Kisbey
Reese, Kathleen, Ebenezer
Reget, Georgina, Pilot Butte
Reich, Ruth, Regina
Reiss, Atholine, Indian Head
Relke, Jane, Regina
Relkey, Pauline, Regina
Rempel, Janis, Regina
Reynard, Edna, Regina
Reynard, Terry, Regina
Rezansoff, Penny, Kamsack
Riddell, Mrs. E., Regina
Robb, Norma Jean, Fort Qu'Appelle
Robin, C., Regina
Robillard, Della, Fort Qu'Appelle
Rodine, Harold, Weyburn
Rollins, Leslie, Regina
Rollins, Tim, Regina
Ross, Louise, Cymric
Ross, Louise, Regina
Russel, M. June, Craven
Ryan, Janet, Tantallon
Sabine, A., Regina
Sali, Claudia, Regina

Sapara, Mrs. Donald, Esterhazy
Sawchyn, Jean, Melville
Sayer, Pat, Regina
Schatz, E., Regina
Schick, Norm, Regina
Schick, Palma, Regina
Schinbein, Beryl, Cabri
Schmidt, Diane, Regina
Schmidt, E.J., Regina
Schneider, Tilly, Regina
Schomburg, Mrs. F., Montmartre
Schroeder, Beulah, Chamberlain
Schuck, Mrs. L. Pearl, Regina
Schuck, Marilyn, Weybrun
Scott, Dorothy, Fillmore
Scott, Lorraine, Regina
Segal, B., Fort Qu'Appelle
Senft, Lois, Punnichy
Serfling, Donna, Regina
Shaw, Marg, Regina
Shea, Barb, Regina
Shepherd, Dave, Regina
Shul, Wendy, Regina
Simmons, J., Regina
Smyth, Pat, Regina
Snell, Muriel, Regina
Sokulski, Don, Regina
Solomon, Mary, Regina
Souillet, Jeannine, Fort Qu'Appelle
Spence, Duncan, Indian Head
Spence, Frances, Indian Head
Springett, Margaret, Moose Jaw
Staite, Caroline, Regina
Staite, John A., Regina
Stakiw, Gail, Regina
Stevenson, Muriel, Regina
Stewart, Olive, Fort Qu'Appelle
Stier, Mary, Regina
Stillwell, Joyce, Regina
Stockton, Marie, Regina
Strandlund, Martha, Broadview
Swanson, C., Regina
Szabo, Mrs. Marge, Regina
Tarr, Maria, Wolseley
Tetlow, Celine, Regina
Thomas, Vi, Weyburn
Thomson, Mrs. M., Regina
Thompson, Barb, Fort Qu'Appelle
Thompson, Shirley, Bienfait
Thoreson, E., Moose Jaw
Thurmeier, Mrs. B., Regina
Tomkins, Penny, Lumsden
Tokevich, Mrs. I., Regina
Tokevich, Mrs. S., Regina
Trafananko, Mrs. Helen, Regina
Trafananko, R.J., Regina

Turcotte, Lynne, Regina
Turner, Donna, Cupar
Turner, M., Regina
Urbanoski, Joyce, Yorkton
Van de Wyer, Doreen, Halbrite
Van Dresar, Leila E., Regina
Vermette, Jo, Regina
Vincze, Maryann, Kipling
Waldbauer, Bob, Regina
Wasylyshen, Mrs. Carol, Yorkton
Watkins, Ron, Fort Qu'Appelle
Wattney, Lorae, Regina
Webb, Mrs. M., Regina
Weimer, Shirley, Kendal
Weir, Hazel, Regina
Weir, Mrs. William, Arcola
Weisberger, Joann, Estevan
Wesson, Marjorie, Regina
Whitney, Gayle, Regina
Wiebe, L., Regina
Wielyoz, Bernice, Moosomin
Wild, Juanita, Regina
Wild, Isobelle, Regina
Wilhelm, Cheryl, Swift Current
Williams, Shirley, Regina
Willoughly, Marjorie, Penzance
Wilson, Mrs. Doreen, Lang
Winsor, Carol, Regina
Wolstenholme, Jackie, Pangman
Woods, Adeline, Swift Current
Woolsey, Carol, Penzance
Woroniak, Lorraine, Wawota
Yaholnitsky, T.P., Regina
Yemen, Dorothy, Regina
Young, Arrol, Arcola
Young, Mrs. Iris, Regina
Yurkowski, Melinda, Regina
Zacharri, Sylvia, Prince Albert
Zacharri, William, Prince Albert
Zacharki, Sylvia, Prince Albert
Zak, Annette, Fir Mountain
Zander, Dennis, Wauchope
Zatylny, Vera, Dysart
Zazada, Jo, Regina
Zepick, Mary, Regina
Zimmer, Sharon, Regina
Zimmerman, Elsie, Regina
Zimmerman, Jeanne, Regina
Zimmerman, Kathy, Regina
Zora, E.E., Regina
Zrymiak, Gail, Ituna
Zurburg, Sandra, Esterhazy
Zyla, Rosella, Fillmore

INDEX

INDEX

141

INDEX

HELPFUL GIFT IDEAS

Household Hints – *Money & Time-Saving Hints* _____ x $12.95 = $_____
Household Hints – *Environment & Energy Hints* _____ x $9.95 = $_____
Cornerstones – *An Artist's History Of The City of Regina* _____ x $15.95 = $_____
HomeTips – *Organizing Strategies For A Streamlined Home Life* ___ x $14.95 = $_____
WorkTips – *Organizing Strategies For A Productive Work Life* _____ x $14.95 = $_____
A Year of Crafts – *For Children & Adults* _____ x $12.95 = $_____
Shipping and handling costs _____ = $_____3.00_____
Subtotal _____ = $_____
In Canada add 7% GST _____ (Subtotal x .07) = $_____
Total enclosed _____ = $_____

U.S. and international orders payable in U.S. funds/Prices subject to change.

NAME: _____
STREET: _____
CITY: _____ PROV./STATE _____
COUNTRY _____ POSTAL/ZIP CODE _____

Please make cheque or money order payable to:

THE LEADER-POST CARRIER FOUNDATION INC.
P.O. Box 2020
1964 Park Street
Regina, Saskatchewan, Canada S4P 3G4

For fund raising or volume purchase prices, contact
THE LEADER-POST CARRIER FOUNDATION INC. at (306) 565-8240.

HELPFUL GIFT IDEAS

Household Hints – *Money & Time-Saving Hints* _____ x $12.95 = $_____
Household Hints – *Environment & Energy Hints* _____ x $9.95 = $_____
Cornerstones – *An Artist's History Of The City of Regina* _____ x $15.95 = $_____
HomeTips – *Organizing Strategies For A Streamlined Home Life* ___ x $14.95 = $_____
WorkTips – *Organizing Strategies For A Productive Work Life* _____ x $14.95 = $_____
A Year of Crafts – *For Children & Adults* _____ x $12.95 = $_____
Shipping and handling costs _____ = $_____3.00_____
Subtotal _____ = $_____
In Canada add 7% GST _____ (Subtotal x .07) = $_____
Total enclosed _____ = $_____

U.S. and international orders payable in U.S. funds/Prices subject to change.

NAME: _____
STREET: _____
CITY: _____ PROV./STATE _____
COUNTRY _____ POSTAL/ZIP CODE _____

Please make cheque or money order payable to:

THE LEADER-POST CARRIER FOUNDATION INC.
P.O. Box 2020
1964 Park Street
Regina, Saskatchewan, Canada S4P 3G4

For fund raising or volume purchase prices, contact
THE LEADER-POST CARRIER FOUNDATION INC. at (306) 565-8240.

Household Hints – Environmental And Energy Hints For Home and Garden

Hundreds of recycling ideas and environmentally friendly alternatives for home and garden, cleaning and maintenance problems. Low-cost, common-sense remedies for everyday problems.

Retail $9.95   96 pages
6" x 9"   40 line drawings   wire coil bound

A Year Of Crafts – For Children And Adults
by Geraldine Hartman

Imaginative craft projects, many with seasonal themes, provide year-round pleasure. Each two-page spread features one child's and one adult's craft with photographs and detailed material and assembly instructions. Suitable for age 6 and up.

Retail $12.95   120 pages
6" x 9"   wire coil bound
                    104 black & white and 32 colored photographs

Cornerstones – An Artist's History Of The City of Regina
by William Argan with Pam Cowan

Historic commercial buildings, schools, churches, hotels, theatres and so much more, Bill Argan's striking illustrations bring the history of Regina alive. Here is a fascinating look at the business, social, political and cultural cornerstones of Regina.

Retail $15.95   144 pages
6" x 9"   over 150 illustrations   perfect bound

HomeTips – Organizing Strategies For A Streamlined Home Life
by Patricia Katz

Family and household organizational tips are the focus here. Patricia Katz has created a helpful, humorous and practical guide to help you balance household demands, with family and personal obligations. Take care of the essentials and get more out of life.

Retail $14.95   128 pages
6" x 9"   fully illustrated   perfect bound

WorkTips – Organizing Strategies For A Productive Work Life
by Patricia Katz

WorkTips will help you and your organization be more productive and effective. Filled with practical suggestions for organizing your time, tackling top priorities, working through others, managing information, mastering technology and conducting business on the run.

Retail $14.95   128 pages
6" x 9"   fully illustrated   perfect bound